Wallace D. Wattles Advanced Vision Guide

How to Fine-Tune Your Vision to Get What You Want in the Shortest Possible Time with the Least Amount of Effort

By Tony Mase
http://www.tonymase.com

Copyright © 2016-2018 Tony Mase – All Rights Reserved

International and federal copyright laws protect the contents of this book.

Any unauthorized copy or use of this material is subject to prosecution under applicable laws.

Disclaimer, Terms of Use Agreement, and Legal Notices

The author and publisher of this book and the accompanying materials have used their best efforts in preparing this book. The author and publisher make no representation or warranties with respect to the accuracy, applicability, fitness, or completeness of the contents of this book. The information contained in this book is strictly for educational purposes. Therefore, if you wish to apply ideas contained in this book, you are taking full responsibility for your actions.

The author and publisher disclaim any warranties (express or implied), merchantability, or fitness for any particular purpose. The author and publisher shall in no event be held liable to any party for any direct, indirect, punitive, special, incidental, or other consequential damages arising directly or indirectly from any use of this material, which is provided "as is" and without warranties.

As always, the advice of a competent legal, tax, accounting, medical, or other appropriate professional should be sought.

The author and publisher do not warrant the performance, effectiveness, or applicability of any sites listed or linked to in this book.

All links are for information purposes only and are not warranted for content, accuracy, or any other implied or explicit purpose.

This book is © copyrighted by Tony Mase and is protected under the US Copyright Act of 1976 and all other applicable international, federal, state, and local laws, with all rights reserved. No part of this book may be copied or changed in any format, sold, or used in any way other than what is outlined within this book under any circumstances without express permission from Tony Mase.

MATERIAL CONNECTION DISCLOSURE: Unless specifically stated otherwise, you should assume the author and publisher of this book have an ownership, affiliate, and/or other material connection to the providers of products and services mentioned in this book and may be compensated when you purchase from a provider.

Table of Contents

Introduction 6

FREE BONUS 9

Chapter 1: How to Determine What's Truly Important to You 10

Chapter 2: The Evolution of a Vision from A to Z 29

Chapter 3: The Evolution of a Vision, a Fictional Case Study 42

Chapter 4: The Evolution of a Vision, a Real-Life Case Study 54

Chapter 5: The Anatomy of an Effective Vision Statement 60

Chapter 6: Six Simple Rules for Creating Your Vision .. 67

Chapter 7: Nine Simple Rules for Wording Your Vision Statement 74

Chapter 8: How to Use the Monthly Expense Calculator 84

Chapter 9: How to Use the Gross-Up Calculator 91

Chapter 10: Purpose and Debt 104

Chapter 11: What to Do Until You Know What You Want 123

Chapter 12: How Long Will It Take to Get What You Want? 127

Conclusion 130

Appendix: Resources 131

About Wallace D. Wattles 134

About Tony Mase.. 137

Other Books from Tony Mase 138

Introduction

Thank you for taking the time to purchase this book!

The *Oxford Advanced American Dictionary*, one of the dictionaries I use in my study of Wallace D. Wattles' writings, defines the word vision, in part, as:

"an idea or a picture in your imagination"

That idea or picture, the way Mr. Wattles used the word in his writings, being of what you want.

Get your vision right and everything else will fall into place. Get it wrong and you have a long, hard road ahead of you filled with anxiety, confusion, frustration, and worry.

Most people, unfortunately, have it wrong... all wrong!

In fact, based on my own experience and that of the many others I've worked with over the years, I can tell you with absolute certainty that most of the troubles people experience when trying to follow Wallace D. Wattles' principles to get what they want in life can be traced back to their vision or lack thereof.

How do you know if your vision is right, *really* right, and, more importantly, how do you fix it if it isn't?

I've written this guide in response to that question.

Based on the writings of Wallace D. Wattles, who's best known for his classic masterpiece *The Science of Getting Rich*, and picking up where my *Wallace D. Wattles Quick Start Guide* leaves off on the subject, this guide will help you fine-tune your vision to get what you want in the shortest possible time with the least amount of effort.

The valuable information contained in it has helped many people, people just like you, to achieve the wealth, health, success, happiness, and love they deserve.

Here are just a few of the many things you'll learn in this comprehensive guide:

- How to determine what's truly important to you and bring your vision and, thus, your life in alignment with those things.

- How to ensure your current next level vision is truly a *next* level vision for you.

- How to properly structure your vision statement for maximum effectiveness.

- Six simple rules for creating your vision.

- Nine simple rules for wording your vision statement.

- How to incorporate debt elimination into your next level vision the right way.

- What to do when you don't know what you want until you do know what you want.

- How long it'll take you to get what you want.

- ... and a whole lot more!

Two important things before we begin:

1. It's expected that you've completed my *Wallace D. Wattles Quick Start Guide,* which is available on

Amazon at http://amzn.to/1mT6Er7, *and* you have a current next level vision in place before beginning this guide. Not a problem if you haven't, but you'll get a whole lot more from it if you have.

> Note: I'll be referring to my *Wallace D. Wattles Quick Start Guide* frequently throughout this manual.
>
> Warning: You'll be reevaluating your current next level vision and, possibly, rewriting your vision statement numerous times during the course of these chapters.

2. Although each chapter of this guide stands on its own, some of them are built, at least somewhat, on the previous ones. Therefore, I suggest completing each chapter, including its action steps, before moving on to the next.

Ready to take your vision and your life to the next level?

Good.

Let's get started then…

Again, thanks for purchasing this book. I hope you find it to be helpful!

Tony Mase

P.S. Don't forget to grab your copy of my FREE BONUS! You'll be able to gain access to it in the next chapter. Enjoy!

FREE BONUS

As a special thank you for taking the time to purchase my book, I'd like to offer you a FREE bonus that's exclusive to my book and blog readers!

The free bonus is my "Constructive Science 101: 3 Keys to Getting What You Want" minicourse.

It's a 4-part email course sent to you every other day in which you'll discover Wallace D. Wattles' simple, easy-to-understand formula for success and lots more.

Plus, you'll get my Constructive Science Newsletter filled with all-new, 100% original self-development tips and strategies to skyrocket your success!

To gain access to this totally free giveaway, head to http://bit.ly/2hnJZEM.

This bonus will get you started in the right direction and seriously help you in the long run. I honestly wish I had this information when I first started – it would've made things so much easier and so much faster.

So, don't hesitate. It's totally free! Go to http://bit.ly/2hnJZEM now and get it for free!

Chapter 1: How to Determine What's Truly Important to You

In the years before I began studying the writings of Wallace D. Wattles, one of the single biggest mistakes I made was wanting things that, looking back on them now, weren't the least bit important to me.

Travel is one that immediately comes to mind. I almost always had a number of goals (back when I set them) on my goals list (back when I had one) to travel to all sorts of exotic places.

The funny part is I'm somewhat of a homebody who doesn't really like to travel all that much. To me travel is more of a hassle than it is fun.

Here's another one. I once had a goal on my list to own a closet full of finely tailored, custom-made suits.

The truth is I'm perfectly happy running around in jeans and a t-shirt.

As a matter of fact, at the very same time I had this goal on my list, I was desperately trying to get to a point in my life where I *didn't* have to wear a suit!

One more, and this one, looking back on it, was downright ridiculous. I had a goal on my list to own a white Lincoln Town Car stretch limousine and have my own personal chauffeur.

What's wrong with that you ask?

Nothing, except there are very few things I like less than being a passenger in a car, especially being a passenger in the back seat of a car.

Plus, at the same time I had this goal on my list, I was trying to eliminate hassles in my life, *not* add more to the ones I already had.

Why then, when I could easily go out and rent a limousine and driver anytime I wanted to, would I want the hassle of owning a car I'd barely, if ever, use and having someone else on my payroll?

Hmm, no wonder I wasn't making any progress toward my goals. They weren't *my* goals! Whose goals were they? I honestly don't know. All I know is they weren't mine.

I guess, for lack of a better explanation, I thought these were things "successful people" did or had, so, since I wanted to be "successful", they were what I should want.

I know that sounds silly, but judging from the questions I get, there are a whole lot of folks out there who think they should want all sorts of things they don't really want at all.

Now, am I saying there's anything wrong with wanting travel, custom-made clothes, or chauffeur-driven limousines? Absolutely not! Unless *you* don't really want those things!

In Chapter 1 of his book *How to Get What You Want*, Wallace D. Wattles wrote the best definition of success I've ever read:

"Getting what you want is success..."

The single, most important key word in Mr. Wattle's definition of success is you. Getting what *you* want is success...

• Not getting what I want...

• Not getting what your father, mother, or other family members want...

• Not getting what your spouse, mate, or significant other wants...

• Not getting what your kids want...

• Not getting what your acquaintances, co-workers, or friends want...

• Not getting what someone else wants you to want...

• Not getting what you think you should want because someone else has it...

Getting what *you* want is success!

Later, in Chapter 1 of *How to Get What You Want*, Mr. Wattles wrote this about success:

"Success is essentially the same, whether it results in the attainment of health, wealth, development or position; success is attainment, without regard to the things attained."

In other words, all success is the same. The only difference is what *you* want.

Getting what *you* want is success!

So, how do you determine what *you* want, and, just as important, how do you separate what *you* really want from what you just think you want?

Simple.

The best way is to determine what's truly important to you and then create your vision of what you want next in your life based on the concepts, feelings, people, and things that're most important to you...

- Not most important to me...

- Not most important to anyone else...

Most important to *you*!

Looking back, had I done that, had I determined what was truly important to me and then decided what I wanted next in my life based on what was most important to me at the time, I'd have saved many, many, *many* long years of emotional trauma, feelings of failure, frustration, and hardship.

As a matter of fact, I'll tell you this, once I began determining what was truly important to me and creating visions of what I wanted next in my life based on what was most important to me at the time, I made more progress in just a couple of years than I had in the previous thirty years combined!

So, with that in mind, let's get on with the process of determining what's truly important to you.

In Chapter 1 of his book *The Science of Getting Rich* ("The Right to Be Rich"), Wallace D. Wattles wrote:

"There are three motives for which we live; we live for the body, we live for the mind, we live for the soul. No one of these is better or holier than the other; all are alike desirable, and no one of the three – body, mind, or soul – can live fully if either of the others is cut short of full life and expression. It is not right or noble to live only for the soul and deny mind or body;

and it is wrong to live for the intellect and deny body or soul."

Absolutely true. However, within those three broad areas of your life, some concepts, feelings, people, and things are more important to you than others, aren't they?

And, all or some of the concepts, feelings, people, and things that're important to you may or may not be important to someone else and vice versa, wouldn't you agree?

We call these concepts, feelings, people, and things *values*.

> Note: You can call them something else if you like, and some folks do, (priorities is one word that immediately comes to mind here), but I like to call them values.

Values are simply the concepts, feelings, people, and things you rate most highly in life. In other words, values are the concepts, feelings, people, and things that're most important to you.

Now, with some seven billion or so people on this planet, you might think there are hundreds, if not thousands or even millions, of potential values.

However, if you were to compile a list of the values of thousands or even tens of thousands of people, chances are you'd find they'd all tend to fall into one of about twenty-five categories:

1. A close relationship with God.

2. A close relationship and/or spending time with children.

3. A close relationship and/or spending time with parents or other family members.

4. A close relationship and/or spending time with spouse, mate, or significant other.

5. A meaningful, rewarding job or career.

6. A sense of accomplishment.

7. Contributing time, knowledge, or money to others.

8. Fame.

9. Free time.

10. Friendships.

11. Happiness.

12. Knowing important or famous people.

13. Meeting the right person.

14. Not having any hassles or problems to deal with.

15. Owning your own business.

16. Peace of mind.

17. Perfect health.

18. Living to an old age.

19. Personal possessions.

20. Power.

21. Respect from others.

22. Retirement.

23. Safety and security.

24. Travel to exciting places.

25. Wealth.

Some combination of these twenty-five values is what makes you *you*. They're what make you tick.

These twenty-five values, in some combination, are what determine what you'll likely do or not do in any given situation.

For example, let's say one of your top values is safety and security. As a matter of fact, let's say safety and security is your number-one value.

How likely is it, regardless of how much you wanted to improve your financial situation, you'd up and quit a safe and secure full-time job and risk it all to start your own full-time business?

Not very likely, is it? So, would it make any sense, whatsoever, to create a next level vision of yourself earning a certain amount of income from your own full-time business? Not really.

Why?

Because wanting a certain amount of income from your own full-time business would be so out of alignment with your number-one value, safety and security, chances are you'd never even think about it, let alone do anything about it.

And, even if you did manage to work up the courage and overcome your fears to take the plunge, how likely is it you'd succeed?

Well, there's no way to know for sure, but odds are you'd be so miserable and so worried because what you did was in such direct conflict with your single most important value, safety and security, that, if for no other reason, you'd probably cause your own demise.

On the other hand, keeping in mind your desire to improve your financial situation, how likely is it you'd consider starting a low-cost, low-risk, home-based business on a part-time basis, while keeping your safe and secure full-time job?

Chances are good, aren't they?

So, would it make sense to create a next level vision of yourself earning a certain amount of income from your own part-time, home-based business?

Absolutely. As a matter of fact, all other factors being equal, chances are good you'd succeed at it.

Why?

Because you'd be working toward improving your financial situation safely and securely in alignment with, instead of in direct conflict with, your number-one value, safety and security.

Now, it's important to note, your values can and will change over time.

In the example above, is it possible you could end up earning so much money in your part-time, home-based business it becomes your new norm for safety and security?

And, is it possible you might get to the point where you feel so safe and secure in your part-time business you'd be perfectly comfortable quitting your full-time job to turn your part-time business into a full-time one?

Of course it is!

This is the value of values.

Rather than constantly beating up on yourself, trying to change who you are, why not figure out who you are by determining what's truly important to you and then working with yourself instead of against yourself?

Trust me, it's a whole heck of a lot simpler than what you've been doing. I know!

As a matter of fact, let me share this with you, once you determine what's truly important to you – your values, and prioritize them in relation to one another, your whole life will get a whole heck of a lot simpler really, really, *really* fast!

How?

For starters, once you determine what your values are and prioritize them, you'll be able to decide, almost instantly, whether you *really* want something or just think you do.

As a rule, those wants in alignment with your top ten values, particularly your top five values, and don't conflict with any of them, will bring you the greatest amount of joy and satisfaction.

Let's look at an example. Remember, at the beginning of this chapter, I told you about the goals I had on my goals list for travel, custom-made clothes, and a chauffeur-driven limousine?

And, remember I said, had I determined what was truly important to me and then decided what I wanted next in my life based on what was important to me at the time, I'd have saved many, many, *many* long years of emotional trauma, feelings of failure, frustration, and hardship?

Well, here's why I said that. After finally figuring out what they were, my top five values are:

1. At-one-ment with God.

2. Perfect health.

3. A close relationship and spending time with my son.

4. Personal freedom.

5. Owning my own highly-profitable, home-based, online business doing what I like to do.

Now, do you see travel anywhere on the list of my top five values? Nope. Travel isn't even on the list of my top ten values. Not important to me.

Do you see custom-made clothes and a chauffeur driven limousine (personal possessions) anywhere on the list of my top five values? Nope. Personal possessions, in general, aren't even on the list of my top ten values. Not important to me either.

Nowadays, I wouldn't waste even the slightest amount of energy and time considering wants like these simply because they aren't in alignment with my top values – the concepts, feelings, people, and things that are most important to me.

Whenever I want something, or at least think I want something, I ask myself these two simple questions:

> 1. To which of my top values will getting this bring me closer to and why?
>
> 2. Will getting this conflict with any of my other top values?

If getting what I want, or at least think I want, doesn't bring me closer to one or more of my top values, particularly my top five values, and/or I can't come up with at least one or more clear, convincing reasons why it will, or if getting what I want, or at least think I want, would conflict with one or more of my top values, particularly my top five values, and I can't come up with a way to resolve this conflict up front, then I drop it. Case closed, over and out. It's that simple!

On the other hand, if getting what I want, or at least think I want, brings me closer to one or more of my top values, particularly my top five values, and I can come up with at least one or more clear, convincing reasons why it will, and if getting what I want, or at least think I want, wouldn't conflict with one or more of my top values, particularly my top five values, or if there's a conflict but I can come up with a way to resolve the conflict up front, then I'll consider adding it to my vision statement or creating a new vision statement including it.

Are you beginning to see how having a prioritized list of your most important values can make your life simpler? I sincerely hope so.

But, easily separating what you really want from what you just think you want is just the first way in which having a prioritized list of your values will make your life simpler. There's another.

Once you determine what your values are and prioritize them, you'll be able to make decisions and evaluate opportunities much more easily and far faster than you ever imagined you could.

For example, let's say the local schools close on a day they're scheduled to be open due to the weather, such as a snowstorm.

Based on my top five values, which I shared with you earlier in this chapter, which of the following do you think I'd do:

   1. Take the day off to spend extra time with my son, or…

   2. Work as I'd planned to do that day.

If you think I'd take the day off to spend extra time with my son, you're right.

It'd take me all of a second to make that decision, and I wouldn't have to think about it twice.

Why?

Because my relationship with my son and the time I spend with him are *far* more important to me than my business.

As a matter of fact, because I *know* my relationship with my son and the time I spend with him are far more important to me than my business, I've built my entire business around my relationship with him and the time I spend with him rather than the other way around.

Here's another example:

Let's say someone were to offer me $10,000,000 a year plus benefits and bonuses to go to work for their company tomorrow.

Based on my top five values, which I shared with you before, do you think I'd accept their offer?

Let's see.

Which of my top five values would accepting this offer bring me closer to…

Would it bring me closer to at-one-ment with God?

No.

Would it bring me closer to perfect health?

No.

Would it bring me closer to a close relationship and spending time with my son?

No.

Would it bring me closer to personal freedom, which I define as the freedom to do whatever I want to do, whenever I want to do it, without money being the deciding factor?

No.

Would it bring me closer to owning my own highly-profitable, home-based, online business doing what I like to do?

No.

On the other hand, would accepting this offer conflict with any of my top five values...

Would it conflict with at-one-ment with God?

Probably not.

Would it conflict with perfect health?

I once heard an entrepreneur defined as someone who'd rather be the captain of a rowboat than the first mate on a battleship. That's me in a nutshell.

Since there's very little I like less than working for someone else, chances are the misery and stress of doing something I don't like to do would destructively impact my health.

Would it conflict with a close relationship and spending time with my son?

More than likely it would, big time! I spend a *serious* amount of time with my son, and working for someone else, on their schedule, would directly impact my ability to spend that time with him.

Would it conflict with personal freedom, which, again, I define as the freedom to do whatever I want to do, whenever I want to do it, without money being the deciding factor?

Accepting the offer to go to work for someone else would eliminate the personal freedom I enjoy right now.

Would it conflict with owning my own highly-profitable, home-based, online business doing what I like to do?

Of course it would.

So if you said no, I wouldn't accept the offer, you're correct.

Do you think raising their offer to $20,000,000 a year, $30,000,000 a year, or even $100,000,000 a year, would make any difference in my decision?

Absolutely not!

Why?

Because I'm crystal clear about what's truly important to me, and I live my life accordingly, and, after completing your action steps for this chapter, you'll be equally as clear about what's truly important to you and on your way to living your life accordingly.

But first, let's summarize:

    1. Values are the concepts, feelings, people, and things that're most important to you.

    2. Once you determine what your values are and prioritize them, you'll be able to decide, almost instantly, whether you *really* want something or you just think you do, and...

3. You'll be able to make decisions and evaluate opportunities much more easily and far faster than you ever imagined you could.

In the next chapter, we'll examine the evolution of a vision from A to Z.

Until then, here are your...

Action Steps

1. Write this list of values on a piece of paper:

- A close relationship with God.

- A close relationship and/or spending time with children.

- A close relationship and/or spending time with parents or other family members.

- A close relationship and/or spending time with spouse, mate, or significant other.

- A meaningful, rewarding job or career.

- A sense of accomplishment.

- Contributing time, knowledge, or money to others.

- Fame.

- Free time.

- Friendships.

- Happiness.

- Knowing important or famous people.

- Meeting the right person.
- Not having any hassles or problems to deal with.
- Owning your own business.
- Peace of mind.
- Perfect health.
- Living to an old age.
- Personal possessions.
- Power.
- Respect from others.
- Retirement.
- Safety and security.
- Travel to exciting places.
- Wealth.

2. Review your written list of values one by one. Circle those that're important to you. Cross off those that aren't.

Feel free to reword the values listed, as necessary, to make them more meaningful to you or more specific to your situation.

For example, you could change (like I did):

A close relationship and/or spending time with children.

To:

A close relationship and spending time with my son.

Add any concepts, feelings, people, and things that're important to you but don't neatly fall into one of the other categories.

> Note: There are no rights or wrongs here. Your values, whatever they may be, are your values.
>
> Warning: I seriously hesitated including my values in this chapter. Why? Because I know some will be tempted to merely copy mine thinking well they worked for Tony, they'll work for me too. Wrong! For this to work, your values need to be just that, *your* values!

3. Prioritize the values you circled from 1 through 10 with 1 being the most important and 10 being the least important.

If you run into values that seem equally important, ask yourself this question:

Which one could I do without?

This will usually identify the stronger of the two values. If that doesn't work, don't get hung up on it, just make a decision. You can always change it later.

> Tip: If you have any trouble whatsoever with this exercise, I suggest repeating it from scratch every two or three days for a week or two, allowing at least a day or two in between sessions to mull it over.
>
> Tip: I *highly* recommend repeating this exercise from time to time, especially when you're about to create a new next level vision or

anytime things just don't seem quite right in your life.

4. List your top ten values, in order of highest priority to lowest priority, on a separate sheet of paper.

> Note: The purpose of this step is to give you a list of your top ten values for easy reference.

5. Using the evaluation questions below, review your next level vision statement to see if it's in alignment with your top ten values:

> 1. To which of my top ten values will realizing this vision bring me closer to and why?
>
> 2. Will realizing this vision conflict with any of my other top ten values? If so, which one(s) and how?
>
> 3. How will I resolve this conflict (or these conflicts)?
>
> 4. How can I associate this vision with my other important values?
>
>> Tip: Answer these questions in writing.
>>
>> Reminder: As a rule, those wants in alignment with your top ten values, particularly your top five values, and don't conflict with any of them, will bring you the greatest amount of joy and satisfaction.

6. If your vision statement isn't in alignment with your top ten values, change it or find a way to bring it into alignment.

Chapter 2: The Evolution of a Vision from A to Z

A while back, a coaching client wrote:

"I really appreciated the story found in Chapter 6..."

Referring to Chapter 6 of my *Wallace D. Wattles Quick Start Guide*...

"... since I have a tendency to want to jump from A to Z. As I pondered what I wanted 'next' I was tempted to think very big... very far from where I am now... but that story pulled me back to just focusing on what is 'next'...

Also, this morning it dawned on me that the 'experience' we gain in going from A to B to C etc. to get to Z is part of why we're here, and helps to educate our desires along the way, so that life is more about 'becoming' and 'experiencing' than 'getting' or 'having'. So there really is no 'Z' only 'next', and 'next' and 'next..."

Very well said and a great springboard for a few important thoughts I'd like to share with you on the subject.

There's a definite tendency, when first starting out in this philosophy, for people to do what, odds are, they've always done and attempt to go from A to Z, or "zero to one hundred" as I called it in Chapter 6 of my *Wallace D. Wattles Quick Start Guide*, in one fell swoop.

> Note: It worked so well the last ten times they did it that way, why not try it again, right? As

> someone once said: "The definition of insanity is doing the same thing over and over again and expecting a different result."

Back in the days before Mr. Wattles came into my life, buying into the "think big" mentality prevalent in just about every self-help book, course, and program out there, that's exactly what I used to do.

> Note: Please don't get me wrong here. Done properly, thinking big has its place, as you'll learn in this chapter. Done improperly though, I can tell you from personal experience, it can lead to total disaster.

There I'd be living in my apartment with a leaky roof, driving my piece of crap car, borrowing from Peter to pay Paul, as they say, just to stay afloat, and, following the advice of one self-help book or another, I'd come up with something totally off-the-wall like wanting to live in a hundred-room mansion, ride around in a chauffeur-driven limousine, and have a million dollars in the bank.

Big boo-boo!

> Note: Though, obviously, I didn't know it at the time. See Chapter 6 of my *Wallace D. Wattles Quick Start Guide* for the reason why if you don't already know it.

Now, why do folks tend to do this?

I've given it a lot of thought over the last several years and, besides following faulty advice or misinterpreting said advice, I've come up with two likely reasons:

> 1. They haven't a clue as to what they want, what they *really* want, and thus, believing it's essential

to their success, they just pick something or some things out of thin air to want that they see other people who they think (the key word here being *think*) are "successful" have, so, they decide they should want it or them too.

> Note: See Chapter 1 of this guide for Mr. Wattles'/my definition of *real* success.

2. Setting what they want so far out there absolves them of the responsibility of doing something *today* to better their situation in life. In other words, it gives them yet one more good excuse to procrastinate taking *action*.

> Note: Their thinking (speaking from personal experience here) usually goes something like this: "Heck, it'll probably take me ten years to do this anyway, so I'll start on it mañana." Mañana never comes, does it?
>
> Sort of reminds me of an old episode of the *Addams Family* in which, after ending up in a business of one sort or another (I forget the storyline now), Uncle Fester said something to the effect of:
>
> *"Now that I'm my own boss, I think I'll give myself the day off."*

There may be other reasons, but, quite frankly, I think it's usually one or the other, or a combination of the two. For me, looking back, it was a combination of the two.

That being said, rather than attempting to go from A to Z, most folks, though not necessarily all, would be *far* better served by a first next level vision that brings them from A to what for many folks would be B:

- A being where they are now.

- B being where they enjoy what I like to refer to as *financial stability*.

Financial stability is that point at which your income fairly easily equals or exceeds your expenses, without incurring new debt to make ends meet.

> Note: This doesn't necessarily mean debt free, it simply means not incurring any new debt.
>
> Once you've stopped the bleeding, so to speak, by reaching the point of financial stability, you can then incorporate the elimination of existing debt, if you choose to do so, into a future next level vision or visions.
>
> In Chapter 10 of this guide, you'll get detailed, step-by-step instructions for doing so.
>
> Note: Please don't interpret this to mean there shouldn't be anything else in your first next level vision statement other than money. You need one or more goodies to entice you.
>
> The story I shared with you in Chapter 7 of my *Wallace D. Wattles Quick Start Guide* is a good example of going from A to B.

It's a real good place to be, and, with the financial pressure off, I think you'll find as I did, at this point, your thinking, as far as what's *truly* important to you and what you *really* want, will have *dramatically* changed.

Things you once thought were so darned important to you won't seem all that important anymore, and things you once thought you couldn't live without, you could care less about now.

Why?

Simple.

Because, in the process of going from A to B, you've grown as a person. In other words, you're not the same *exact* person you were at A that you now are at B.

And, this new you, with your added insight and increased ability, confidence, and faith, will be capable of seeing and going next *not* from B to C, but from B to D.

Then, for the exact same reason, from D to H, H to P, and so on.

> Note: The more financially stable you are and the greater your level of belief and faith, based on past experience, the bigger you can make your next level vision without it backlashing on you.

Thus, this client's ah-ha of:

"... the 'experience' we gain in going from A to B to C etc. to get to Z is part of why we're here, and helps to educate our desires along the way, so that life is more about 'becoming' and 'experiencing' than 'getting' or 'having'."

Is spot-on!

Because, as I wrote in my reply to her:

"I think you'll find, as I have, that when you go from A to B, the person you've become in the process of getting to B has a dramatically different perspective than the person you were at A and thus at B your C or D might be totally different than anything you could have possibly imagined at A."

> Note: That's why it's so important to reevaluate what's important to you (your values) whenever you reach a new level before deciding on a next one. See Chapter 1 of this guide for details.

The same holds true at any stage of this continuum.

> Note: Personally, and this may or may not hold true for you, I've noticed, the farther along this continuum I progress, the less importance I place on the material and the more importance I place on the non-material.
>
> At one time in my life (most of it, in fact), my ends were always in the realm of the physical, whereas, nowadays, I look at the physical as simply means (tools) to non-physical ends.
>
> Tip: A good test to see if a potential next level vision is right for you at any given point in time is to try it on, so to speak, just as you would a piece of clothing before buying it.
>
> Simply project yourself into it mentally, imagining it as your already accomplished reality, and examine how you feel.
>
> If it fits well, if it feels comfortable, if it feels good, and/or it gives you the warm fuzzies, as

they say, just thinking about it, then odds are it's right for you at this point in your life.

On the other hand, if it doesn't fit well (it's too tight or too loose), if, for whatever reason, it feels uncomfortable, if it feels bad, and/or you get this gnawing or sick feeling in the pit of your gut just thinking about it, then odds are it's not right for you at this point in your life, and it's time to go back to the drawing board.

Another thing to watch out for here is a so what or who cares feeling. Not a good sign.

By the way, this little test also works *extremely* well when you're torn between two (or more) potential next level visions that both feel good when you try them on.

Simply try each of them on (you may have to go back and forth between them several times) and see which one feels best. Chances are the one that feels best is the better choice for you at this point in your life.

With that, in reference to the second part of her ah-ha:

"So there really is no 'Z' only 'next', and 'next' and 'next'..."

A couple of quotes from the big guy come to mind here.

First, In Chapter 1 of his book *The Science of Being Great* ("Any Person May Become Great"), Mr. Wattles wrote:

"The purpose of life for man is growth, just as the purpose of life for trees and plants is growth. Trees and plants grow automatically and along fixed lines; man can grow as he will. Trees and plants can only develop certain possibilities and characteristics; man can develop any power which is or has been shown by any person, anywhere. Nothing that is possible in spirit is impossible in flesh and blood. Nothing that man can think is impossible in action. Nothing that man can imagine is impossible of realization.

Man is formed for growth, and he is under the necessity of growing.

It is essential to his happiness that he should continuously advance. Life without progress becomes unendurable, and the person who ceases from growth must either become imbecile or insane. The greater and more harmonious and well-rounded his growth, the happier man will be."

> Note: If you've ever pondered the purpose of life or the meaning of it all, there it is, plain and simple: "The purpose of life for man is growth..."

Second, in Chapter 14 of *The Science of Getting Rich* ("The Impression of Increase"), he wrote:

"The desire for increase is inherent in all nature; it is the fundamental impulse of the universe. All human activities are based on the desire for increase; people are seeking more food, more clothes, better shelter, more luxury, more beauty, more knowledge, more pleasure – increase in something, more life.

Every living thing is under this necessity for continuous advancement; where increase of life ceases, dissolution and death set in at once.

Man instinctively knows this, and hence he is forever seeking more. This law of perpetual increase is set forth by Jesus in the parable of the talents; only those who gain more retain any; from him who hath not shall be taken away even that which he hath."

> Note: If you're not familiar with it or need a refresher, here's Jesus' parable of the talents from the twenty-fifth chapter of the Book of Matthew in the King James Version of the Bible:
>
> *"14For the kingdom of heaven is as a man travelling into a far country, who called his own servants, and delivered unto them his goods.*
>
> *15And unto one he gave five talents, to another two, and to another one; to every man according to his several ability; and straightway took his journey.*
>
> *16Then he that had received the five talents went and traded with the same, and made them other five talents.*
>
> *17And likewise he that had received two, he also gained other two.*
>
> *18But he that had received one went and digged in the earth, and hid his lord's money.*
>
> *19After a long time the lord of those servants cometh, and reckoneth with them.*

20And so he that had received five talents came and brought other five talents, saying, Lord, thou deliveredst unto me five talents: behold, I have gained beside them five talents more.

21His lord said unto him, Well done, thou good and faithful servant: thou hast been faithful over a few things, I will make thee ruler over many things: enter thou into the joy of thy lord.

22He also that had received two talents came and said, Lord, thou deliveredst unto me two talents: behold, I have gained two other talents beside them.

23His lord said unto him, Well done, good and faithful servant; thou hast been faithful over a few things, I will make thee ruler over many things: enter thou into the joy of thy lord.

24Then he which had received the one talent came and said, Lord, I knew thee that thou art an hard man, reaping where thou hast not sown, and gathering where thou hast not strawed:

25And I was afraid, and went and hid thy talent in the earth: lo, there thou hast that is thine.

26His lord answered and said unto him, Thou wicked and slothful servant, thou knewest that I reap where I sowed not, and gather where I have not strawed:

27Thou oughtest therefore to have put my money to the exchangers, and then at my coming I should have received mine own with usury.

28Take therefore the talent from him, and give it unto him which hath ten talents.

29For unto every one that hath shall be given, and he shall have abundance: but from him that hath not shall be taken away even that which he hath.

30And cast ye the unprofitable servant into outer darkness: there shall be weeping and gnashing of teeth."

Hmm, I don't know what that "gnashing of teeth" stuff is all about, but it sure doesn't sound like a good thing to me.

Now, I know this parable may sound downright cruel, however, this is how the Universe works!

As Mr. Wattles wrote elsewhere, there are two forces in Nature constantly at work simultaneously, construction and destruction. One *always* being the dominant force.

Thus, to put it bluntly, you're either growing or you're dying. There's no standing still! Because when construction ceases, destruction *automatically* becomes the dominant force and, as Mr. Wattles put it so well, "... dissolution and death set in at once."

Thus, even if there were a Z, you don't ever want to get there!

Why?

Simple:

"... where increase of life ceases, dissolution and death set in at once."

> Note: Think about it. How many people have you known in your life, whose work was a major part of their life, who, though there was absolutely nothing wrong with them when they retired, retired only to pass on a very short time thereafter. I've known many! My dad, sadly, being one of them.

So, with that in mind, as a person I once knew used to say:

Go and grow!

> Note: Reminds me of something I heard Jim Rohn say at a seminar I attended many years ago. I forget the subject, but the question was how tall does a tree grow? The answer? As tall as it can!

In the next chapter, we'll examine a fictional case study of how one gal's vision evolved over time.

Until then, here are your...

Action Steps

1. In light of what you learned from this chapter, reevaluate your next level vision, then...

2. Refine or revise it as necessary.

> Note: Your primary objective in this and the next two chapters is to examine where you are

in the evolutionary process and ensure your current next level vision is truly a *next* level vision for you.

Chapter 3: The Evolution of a Vision, a Fictional Case Study

Before we begin, I think it's important for you to know that although this is a fictional case study, its "star", if you will, a young lady whom I've named Shannon, is actually a fictional composite of two or three real people I've worked with over the last several years.

So, although this is a fictional case study, revolving around a fictional character, it's based on real-life experiences.

> Note: This chapter is based on Wallace D. Wattles' story of "a very poor man, living in a rented house, and having only what he earned from day to day" (see Chapter 6 of my *Wallace D. Wattles Quick Start Guide*) and how I create my visions.
>
> It'll show you *exactly* how, at any given point, to decide what you want next in your life and create an effective vision statement for getting it, thus, providing you with a simple model you can use to create next level visions under a variety of circumstances.

With that, let's begin...

Shannon is twenty years old and living at home with her parents. She recently dropped out of college and isn't working.

Obviously, Shannon's parents were disappointed in her decision to leave school because they'd really like to see her make something of herself.

And, they're not alone. Shannon would really like to make something of herself too! The trouble is she's not sure what.

You see, like a lot of folks, Shannon feels sort of lost. She knows she wants more out of life, but she's just not sure what. However, she does know what's important to her right now.

She'd like to have a full-time job so she'll have income of her own.

Up until now, other than a few odd part-time jobs while she was going to school, she's been dependent on her parents for her financial needs and wants.

Since she doesn't know exactly what she wants to do, she's not real fussy as to the kind of job right now as long as it's enjoyable to her and not illegal or immoral.

Shannon would also like to own her own car. She's been using her mother's car as she needs it, but she'd really like the independence of having her own car.

Although she doesn't know specifically which make and model right now, she does know she wants to buy or lease a new car, not a used car.

Eventually, she'd also like to move out of her parent's home and live on her own, but this isn't a high priority for her right now.

So, right now, Shannon's highest priorities, her top values (see Chapter 1 of this guide for details) are:

   1. An enjoyable job.

   2. Owning a new car.

Now that she's clear about what's most important to her, Shannon's next step is to determine specifically what she wants next in her life and the exact amount of income she'll need to get what she wants and live the life she wants to live next.

For starters, she wants to own a new car. So, she goes car shopping and picks out a make and model she likes.

Shannon learns she can lease the car she likes, with no money down, for $300 a month. She also learns it'll cost her $100 a month for car insurance and another $100 a month for property taxes on the car.

Shannon now knows that to get her new car, she'll need $500 a month in income to pay for it ($300 a month for the lease payment + $100 a month for car insurance + $100 a month for property taxes = $500 a month).

In addition, Shannon's in credit card and student loan debt to the tune of $5,000, $2,500 in credit card debt and $2,500 in student loan debt.

Her minimum required payment on her credit card debt is $100 a month, and her minimum required payment on her student loan debt is $50 a month, both of which she's currently paying by borrowing from Peter to pay Paul, digging herself into the hole even further.

She's decided as soon as she starts working and has income, she's going to pay for whatever she wants by cash, check, debit card, or electronic transfer. No more charging anything!

And, since she doesn't want to be in debt forever, she's decided she wants to pay an extra $50 a month, over and above the minimum required payments due, to pay off her debts faster.

She's decided to start by applying the $50 a month to her credit card debt as it has the highest interest rate.

So, there's another $200 a month in income she'll need ($150 a month to make the minimum required payments + $50 a month for debt elimination = $200 a month).

Then, Shannon wants to have some spending money for clothes, eating out, gas for her new car, going out, etc. She determines that $400 a month will be adequate for that right now.

Plus, besides helping around the house, which she's been doing, Shannon wants to give her parents $100 a month room and board, which they've agreed to and intend on saving for her.

Let's summarize, to get what she wants and live the life she wants to live next, Shannon needs to earn:

- $100 a month for room and board.

- $100 a month for property taxes for her car.

- $150 a month for credit card payments ($100 a month for the minimum required payment + $50 a month for debt elimination).

- $300 a month for her car payment.

- $50 a month for her minimum required student loan payment.

- 100 a month for car insurance.

- $400 a month to spend anyway she likes.

Plugging these numbers into the appropriate categories of the Monthly Expense Calculator at:

http://fourhourworkweek.com/expense-calculator

Shannon determines that, with a 30% buffer, she needs to earn a total of $1,560 a month.

> Note: In Chapter 8 of this guide, you'll get detailed, step-by-step instructions for using the Monthly Expense Calculator.

However, she really needs to earn more than that, doesn't she?

Why?

Simple.

Living in the United States and in a state that has an income tax, Shannon must take into account federal and state income, Medicare, and Social Security taxes that'll be deducted from what she earns.

In reality, to take home $1,560 a month, using the Gross-Up Calculator at:

http://www.paycheckcity.com/calculator/grossup/

> Warning: This site's been a bit finicky as of late. If you have any trouble accessing the Gross-Up Calculator at the link I just gave you, go to http://www.paycheckcity.com and click on Gross Up Calculator near the top of the page. Also, you should know, this site doesn't like ad blockers and, if you use one, you may need to

disable it for this site in order to use the calculator.

Shannon determines she'll need to earn $1,927.99 a month gross income (Shannon lives in the state of California, is single, is her own dependent, and is assuming, at this point, she'll be paid weekly).

> Note: Due to changes in tax rates and other variables, this amount may be different than what the calculator would return today.

> Note: In Chapter 9 of this guide, you'll get detailed, step-by-step instructions for using the Gross-Up Calculator.

Shannon rounds this figure up to $2,000 a month.

So, what Shannon wants next in her life is to earn $2,000 a month from a job she enjoys and to have a new car, thus her vision statement reads:

"I am earning $2,000 a month from a job I enjoy while I enjoy driving my new _____."

Following the instructions in my *Wallace D. Wattles Quick Start Guide*, Shannon obtains these things in a few months.

Now what?

Shannon reevaluates and discovers, just as you will, now that the financial pressure is off and she's gotten to the next level, her priorities have changed, and she's able to think much more clearly about what she really wants.

For one, now that she's a contributing member of the household and understands what her parents have to do to earn a living, she's experiencing a closer relationship with her parents, one she really enjoys.

And, she's discovered she really rather enjoys living at home with her parents, and, of course, they enjoy having her there, so, at least for right now, moving out and living on her own is no longer a priority for her.

Shannon's also discovered that, although she enjoys her job, she really doesn't like working for someone else and would much rather be her own boss.

In addition, after driving high-mileage used cars her whole life, Shannon really likes driving her new car, so much so, she decides she wants to get a new one every two or three years so she'll always be driving a new car.

So, after she reevaluates, Shannon's top values are:

1. A close relationship and spending time with her parents.

2. Owning her own business.

3. Owning a new car.

Now, during her free time, Shannon's been going to tag sales, something she's been doing with her mom since she was a kid and something she really enjoys doing.

And, just for the heck of it, she listed several of her finds on eBay, which sold for a substantial profit.

That's gotten Shannon to thinking maybe she could start her own business selling on eBay:

• It's something she really enjoys doing.

- She seems to be good at it.

- There'd be little, if any, risk involved as she could start her business part time while keeping her full-time job.

- She already has a computer, monitor, and printer that her parents gave her one Christmas and a high-speed internet connection, so she doesn't need much to get started other than maybe some shipping supplies.

- Because she's been putting money in the bank for opportunities, she has the money, if she needs it, to buy inventory and anything else she might need to get started with.

- She'd have practically no overhead as her parents have agreed to let her use a spare room at home to run her business out of.

So, Shannon decides what she wants next in her life is to earn $2,500 a month from her full-time job and her part-time eBay business ($2,000 a month from her full-time job plus $500 a month from her eBay business) while she lives at home with her parents and drives her new car.

Using the Salary Paycheck Calculator at:

http://www.paycheckcity.com/calculator/salary/

> Warning: This site's been a bit finicky as of late. If you have any trouble accessing the Salary Calculator at the link I just gave you, go to http://www.paycheckcity.com and click on Salary Calculator near the top of the page. Also, you should know, this site doesn't like ad blockers and, if you use one, you may need

disable it for this site in order to use the calculator.

Shannon estimates with a gross income of $2,500 a month, she'll have, after taxes, a net income of $1,973.10 a month.

> Note: Due to changes in tax rates and other variables, this amount may be different than what the calculator would return today.

> Note: The Salary Paycheck Calculator is essentially the Gross-Up Calculator in reverse.

What's Shannon going to do with that $1,973.10 a month? She's already decided.

Of course, she still has her lease payment, insurance, and property taxes on her new car that total $500 a month.

However, in addition to that, Shannon's decided to give herself a raise.

She'd been allotting $400 a month for personal expenses (spending money for clothes, eating out, gas for her new car, going out, etc.).

She's decided to increase that to $500 a month.

Plus, because she'll be using an extra room at her parents' house and will probably be eating at home more, Shannon wants to increase the amount of room and board she gives her parents from $100 a month to $500 a month.

The remaining $473.10 a month, her buffer, Shannon intends to bank for future opportunities.

So, at her new next level of income, Shannon intends to allot:

- $500 a month for room and board.
- $100 a month for property taxes for her car.
- $300 a month for her car payment.
- $100 a month for car insurance.
- $500 a month to spend anyway she likes.
- $473.10 a month (her buffer) for opportunity money.

For a total of $1,973.10 a month, her new net income after taxes.

What happened to the $200 a month she'd allotted for debt elimination you ask?

Good question.

Because as soon as she had some income coming in, Shannon began paying for whatever she bought by cash, check, debit card, or electronic transfer, and because Shannon worked a lot of overtime over the last several months and very wisely added the money she earned by working the overtime to her minimum monthly payments and the $50 a month she decided to add to the payments, Shannon has eliminated her credit card and student loan debt and is now debt-free!

Shannon's new next level vision statement reads:

"I am earning $2,500 a month from my job and my eBay business while I enjoy living at home with my parents and driving my new _____."

And, once again, following the instructions in my *Wallace D. Wattles Quick Start Guide*, Shannon realizes this new next level in a few months.

Now what?

Shannon reevaluates again.

Unlike the last time she reevaluated, her values haven't changed. Shannon's top three values are still:

    1. A close relationship and spending time with her parents.

    2. Owning her own business.

    3. Owning a new car.

However, this working for someone else thing is really getting old to Shannon.

Her part-time eBay business is doing extremely well and she absolutely loves doing it, so she decides she wants it to be her full-time business replacing her full-time job.

So, what Shannon decides she wants next in her life is to earn $2,500 a month from her eBay business while she lives at home with her parents and drives her new car.

Thus, her new next level vision statement reads:

"I am earning $2,500 a month from my eBay business while I enjoy living at home with my parents and driving my new _____."

The only thing Shannon wants to change at her new next level is the source of her income, nothing else.

She intends to continue working at her full-time job while building her part-time eBay business, slowly cutting back on the hours she works at her job as her eBay business income increases until she completely replaces the income from her job with the income from her eBay business.

Once again, following the instructions in my *Wallace D. Wattles Quick Start Guide*, Shannon realizes this new next level in a matter of months.

Well, Shannon sure has come a long way in a fairly short period of time, hasn't she?

What's next for Shannon?

That's up to Shannon of course, but, whatever it is, Shannon knows *exactly* how to get it!

In the next chapter, we'll examine a real-life case study of how my vision has evolved over time.

Until then, here are your...

Action Steps

1. In light of what you learned from this chapter, reevaluate your next level vision, then...

2. Refine or revise it as necessary.

> Reminder: Your primary objective in this chapter, as in the previous chapter and the next one, is to examine where you are in the evolutionary process and ensure your current next level vision is truly a *next* level vision for you.

Chapter 4: The Evolution of a Vision, a Real-Life Case Study

In Chapter 7 of my *Wallace D. Wattles Quick Start Guide*, I shared with you my very first vision (minus the personal details):

"I am earning a net income of $_____ a month from my _____ business while I enjoy driving my new _____ and spending unlimited time with my son."

In this chapter, I'll share with you how this vision has evolved over the years to get to the point where it is today.

My intention, in writing this chapter, is to provide you with several, proven, real-life examples you can use as models when revising your vision as it and you evolve.

After I got the new car I wanted and had the income from my business coming in in such a way I was able to spend unlimited time with my son, I took another long, hard look at my life and decided what I wanted next was my own home.

I'd spent my entire adult life living in apartments.

The last one was in an apartment complex, which, although it was a nice place to live at one time, due to the neglect of the owners and the complex's management, had deteriorated over the years I'd lived there to the point of what I can best describe as a dump.

I'll spare you all the gory details, but, let it suffice to say, I wanted out, bad, *real* bad!

Only this time, based on my increased level of faith, I decided it wasn't going to be out to another apartment, I decided it was going to be out to my own home, something I wouldn't have even considered to be in the realm of possibility just a few short months before.

Using the exact same procedure that I outlined in Chapter 7 of my *Wallace D. Wattles Quick Start Guide*, I created this vision for my life (minus the personal details):

"I am earning a net income of $_____ a month from my _____ business while I enjoy living in my _____, spending unlimited time with my son, and being in absolutely perfect health."

Now, notice I added a health component to my vision.

It was around this time I'd begun seriously reading and studying Mr. Wattles' health writings in which he stressed the importance of forming a clear conception of being in perfect health, so I built this conception of being in perfect health right into my vision.

Long story short, it was just a matter of time until I had the home I wanted and my health was improving.

What next?

Good question and one I had as well.

You see, it was at this point I ran into a bit of a roadblock.

Now that my business income had increased to the point where I could stay self-employed and I wasn't struggling financially anymore, I was spending unlimited time with my son, I had the car, I had the home, and my health was improving, quite frankly, I was really rather comfortable at this point and didn't know what, if anything, I wanted next in my life.

So, what did I do?

Simple.

I continued doing all I could do each day, doing each separate thing in an efficient manner, moving forward toward more life, with the full faith that what I was to do next in my life would be revealed to me when the time was right for me to know it.

And guess what?

It was!

Early one morning, at 3:00 AM (for some strange reason the Universe likes to reveal things to me at 3:00 AM), I awoke from a sound sleep with the answer.

What I wanted next in my life was to share the many rare books and articles by Wallace D. Wattles I'd collected with other people in the form of ebooks so they could enjoy the same wonderful benefits from Mr. Wattles' writings that I had.

So, once again, using the exact same procedure that I outlined in Chapter 7 of my *Wallace D. Wattles Quick Start Guide*, I created this vision for my life (minus the personal details):

"I am earning a net income of $_____ a month from my ebook business while I enjoy unlimited time with my son and absolutely perfect health."

Now, three important notes about this vision:

First, the amount of income I wanted to earn wasn't a whole heck of a lot more than what I was earning at the time. The big change was a total change in *how* that income came in.

Second, notice, if you will, I didn't have any big material thing in this vision.

Why not?

Simple.

Because there wasn't really any material thing I wanted that I didn't already have or couldn't just go out and buy if I really needed or wanted it.

Third, and this is really important for you to understand, I hadn't the slightest clue as to how this major change was going to happen!

You see:

- I barely knew what an ebook was let alone know how to make one.

- I didn't know the first thing about how to build a website and, even if I did, I hadn't the slightest clue as to how one got it to appear on the internet.

- I knew nothing about doing business online or internet marketing, nothing, absolutely nothing!

All I had at the time were the most very basic of computer skills.

However, none of that stopped me.

Based on my past experiences, my last two next level visions that had become my reality, I had complete, one-hundred percent, total faith (the key word here is *faith*) that *all* the necessary answers would come to me as I needed them, and, sure enough, obviously, they did!

Now, as this vision evolved (I occasionally revised the income figure in it) and materialized, I went on my merry way expanding my ebook business and freely sharing what I'd learned from Mr. Wattles' writings with my customers and newsletter subscribers for a few years.

However, during this whole time, one thing kept nagging at me in the back of my mind.

I knew from the thousands of questions I'd received and answered, back when I was still able to do so, that there were a whole lot of folks out there who needed help applying Mr. Wattles' philosophy to their lives, far more help than I could provide in ebooks, newsletter articles, and doing things the way I was doing them.

Something more was needed, I just didn't know what.

So, I sat down and created a new vision (minus the personal details):

"I am earning a net income of $_____ a month from my online businesses while I enjoy unlimited personal freedom, unlimited time with my son, and absolutely perfect health."

Essentially expanding my horizons as to the possibilities of what I could do to provide the help that was needed and adding one other very important element to my vision that I'd discovered was extremely important to me, personal freedom.

To me, personal freedom is the freedom to do whatever I want to do, whenever I want to do it, without money being the deciding factor.

Another long story short, here we are today!

In the next chapter, you'll learn the anatomy of an effective vision statement.

Until then, here are your...

Action Steps

1. In light of what you learned from this chapter, reevaluate your next level vision, then...

2. Refine or revise it as necessary.

> Reminder: Your primary objective in this chapter, as in the last two, is to examine where you are in the evolutionary process and ensure your current next level vison is truly a *next* level vision for you.

Chapter 5: The Anatomy of an Effective Vision Statement

Since I first began creating visions and vision statements (see Chapter 7 of my *Wallace D. Wattles Quick Start Guide* for details), I've experimented on and off over the years with various ways of doing it only to find myself returning each and every time to pretty much exactly how I did it in the very beginning.

Today my next level vision statement (minus the personal details), which, structurally anyway, is but a very slightly refined version of what I began with, looks like this:

I am earning a net income of $_____ a month through _____ while I enjoy unlimited personal freedom, regular quality time with my son, and absolutely perfect health at my ideal body weight of_____ pounds.

> Note: See Chapter 4 of this guide to see how my vision has evolved over the years since I first began reading and studying Mr. Wattles' writings.

Short, sweet, simple, and to the point!

> Note: I've heard of people's vision statements rambling on for pages, sometimes filling entire notebooks.

How the heck can they remember all that?

The answer is, regardless of what they may think, they can't.

My advice is don't let that be you. Keep your vision statement short, sweet, simple, and to the point.

Let's examine it piece by piece:

1. I...

I always begin my vision statements with a simple first person "I" and suggest you do as well.

2. ... am earning...

Alternatives here include:

- ... earn...
- ... am making...
- ... make...

And other variations thereof.

However you choose to phrase this, the key here is that it be present tense. In other words, it needs to be in the context of *now*.

> Note: After experimenting with the use of "am making" and "make" in my vision statements, I've returned to the use of "am earning" as, for whatever reason, it seems to be more effective.

3. ... a net income of...

As I noted in my *Wallace D. Wattles Quick Start Guide*, a net income (or net profit) to someone who's self-employed, as I am, is the equivalent of gross income (pre-tax income) to someone who works for someone else.

I include this qualifier in my vision statement as it helps me mentally experience the end result I want more clearly. It or a similar phrase is only necessary if it helps you do the same.

4. ... $_____ a month...

This is where you plug in the specific amount of monthly income it'll take to finance the acquisition of what you want and the lifestyle you want to live next in your life.

> Note: For detailed instructions on how to do this, I refer you to Chapter 7 of my *Wallace D. Wattles Quick Start Guide* and Chapters 8, 9, and 10 of this guide.
>
> Note: Why monthly and not yearly income here?
>
> Two main reasons:
>
> First, it's far easier for you to believe, process, and mentally experience earning the smaller monthly income figure than it is the larger annual income figure.
>
> In other words, it's far easier for you to believe, process, and mentally experience earning $5,000 a month than it is $60,000 a year.
>
> Second, and closely related to the first, because you pay most of your bills and/or make most of your payments on a monthly basis (rent, mortgage, utilities, car payment(s), credit card

payment(s), etc., for example), using a monthly income figure as the cornerstone of your vision allows you to break bigger expenses into smaller, more believable, monthly expenses.

For example, it's much easier for you to believe you can make a $500 a month car payment or a $1,500 a month mortgage payment than it is for you to believe you can come up with $20,000 for the car or $150,000 for the home.

5. ... through...

Alternatives here would be:

- ... as a...
- ... as an...
- ... from...
- ... from my...

And other variations thereof.

This is where you put how you want to earn the specific amount of monthly income it'll take to finance the acquisition of what you want and the lifestyle you want to live next in your life.

Although I don't overly recommend it, you can include more than one source of income here.

> Note: For the sake of simplicity, ease in experiencing it mentally, and in order to facilitate the maintenance of focus, although it may have multiple streams of revenue within it,

I prefer to think in terms of *one* source of income when it comes to my vision statement.

On the other hand, if you haven't a clue as to exactly how you want to earn this money, you can leave this piece of your vision statement out until it comes to you.

6. ... while I enjoy...

Here's where you put the highlights, so to speak, of specifically what you want the income for and anything else you want at this next level of your life.

Although you can have more or less if you really want to, I strongly suggest you limit yourself to no more than three things here:

1. A material biggie...

2. A non-material biggie, and...

3. Something about your health.

Speaking of which...

7. ... at my ideal body weight of _____ pounds.

I've found if I don't put something in my vision statement about an ideal body weight, I tend to get a bit sloppy in my eating habits and, as a result, my weight tends to creep up, thus the inclusion of this statement.

If, for whatever the reason, body weight is important to you, I'd definitely recommend adding this component to your vision statement. If it's not, then no need to include it.

With that...

That's it!

Again, short, sweet, simple, and to the point.

> Note: You'll notice I don't have a material biggie in my current next level vision statement.
>
> Why not, you ask?
>
> Simple.
>
> I've reached a point in my life where I can pretty much just go out and buy anything I really need or want (my material needs and wants are fairly simple nowadays; once I had the money to buy them, most of the things I always thought I wanted, I discovered I didn't really want at all) and non-material things like my work (the income component of my vision statement being more of a scorecard than anything else now), my freedom, time with my son, and my health are far more important to me than material things.
>
> Odds are, if you're not there already, you're going to reach this point in your life as well.

A well-constructed vision statement, based on what's *truly* important to you and what you *really* want, is the single, most important factor in your getting what you want...

Don't leave home without it!

In the next chapter, you'll learn six simple rules for creating your vision.

Until then, here are your...

Action Steps

1. Get your vision statement out.

2. Review this chapter and, piece by piece, compare the anatomy of my vision statement with yours.

3. Refine or revise your vision statement as necessary.

Chapter 6: Six Simple Rules for Creating Your Vision

There are six simple rules you absolutely, positively must follow in order to create your vision properly.

1. Your vision must be balanced.

At an absolute, bare minimum, your vision should include a specific amount of monthly income you want to earn and at least one thing you want to do or have with that income.

A specific amount of monthly income, in and of itself, is difficult to experience emotionally in your imagination.

On the other hand, wanting something without the income to pay for it is just setting yourself up for frustration and/or going into debt.

2. The individual components of your vision must be consistent with one another.

Think of your vision as a kind of jigsaw puzzle and each component of your vision as a piece of the puzzle.

When all the pieces of the puzzle (the components of your vision) are put together, they should form one balanced, consistent picture of what you want next in your life – the next level you want to be at.

The components of your vision should fit together to form a picture that makes sense to you. It doesn't have to make sense to me, or to anyone else, but it does have to make sense to you.

The amount of monthly income you want to earn should be consistent with what you want to have and/or do with that income, and what you want to have and/or do should be consistent with the amount of monthly income you want to earn.

Notice that we're not talking here about creating short-range, mid-range, and long-range visions, but one balanced, consistent vision of what you want next in your life. After you realize it, you'll reevaluate and then create a new, higher, next level vision.

3. Your vision must be believable.

Your vision should be big enough to turn you on emotionally and cause you to feel enthusiastic and excited whenever you think about it.

However, it shouldn't be so big it seems absolutely ridiculous, downright impossible, or totally unimaginable to you.

Only you can decide what believable is for you.

Here's a good test to help you decide:

Close your eyes and imagine yourself as already having that which your vision calls for, as clearly and vividly as you can. Then, ask yourself how it feels now that you have what you want.

If it feels good, if you feel excited, if you get goose bumps or the warm fuzzies just thinking about it, then odds are your vision is believable to you.

On the other hand, if it doesn't feel good, if you get a sick feeling in the pit of your gut, if you find yourself with "yeah right" going off in your head as you think about it, then odds are it isn't.

Most people are inclined to play it safe and create their vision too low.

Don't sell yourself short! You have an unlimited amount of previously untapped power within you and your vision is going to help you release that power.

However, there's a very clear and ever-present danger in creating your vision too high, of trying to go from zero to one hundred in one fell swoop.

If your vision is beyond what you believe is possible for you right now, if it's so high you can't easily project yourself into it and imagine it as an already accomplished fact, then creating that vision will have little or no effect on your progress.

As a matter of fact, it could have exactly the opposite effect!

4. Your vision must be specific.

The more detailed your vision is the better.

It's not enough to want more income.

Specifically, how much monthly income do you want to earn?

If a home is part of your vision, what style is it, how many rooms does it have, what's its floor plan, how's it landscaped, how much does it cost?

What are some of the special extras about the home that are very important to you? Do you want an entertaining area, a special kind of kitchen, an in ground swimming pool, a fireplace?

If a car is part of your vision, decide on the exact make, model, body style, color, and any other details that're important to you.

Go to a dealer for a brochure so you can get a detailed picture of just what the car looks like. Take the car for a test drive so you'll know exactly what it feels like.

If a vacation trip is part of your vision, decide exactly where you want to go and exactly how long you want to be there.

Get some travel folders. Look through magazines or on the internet for pictures.

The more specific your vision is, the easier it'll be for you to project yourself into it and experience it as an already accomplished fact in your imagination.

5. Your vision must be kept confidential.

Discuss your vision only with those individuals who're going to be directly involved in the attainment and/or enjoyment of it.

For example, if your vision includes getting a home, get everyone who'll be living in that home involved in creating it so you'll all be focused on the exact same vision of it.

Not only will you obtain it much faster this way, but when you move into the new home, it'll be an exciting day for everyone because they'll all be moving into *their* new home, not just *your* new home.

However, don't make the mistake of telling everyone you know about your vision of a new home.

Most people are absolutely convinced they can't get what they want, and they're extremely jealous and downright resentful of anyone who, even for a moment, dares to think they can.

Thus, by sharing your vision with them, all you'll be doing is setting yourself up for an avalanche of destructive input that you certainly don't need or want.

Consider yourself warned!

6. Your vision must be stated in the present tense.

After you've decided on the components of your vision, defined them as clearly and specifically as possible, and checked to make sure they're consistent with one another, translate them into one simple, brief, positive, present tense statement – your vision statement.

In the next chapter, you'll learn nine simple rules for wording your vision statement.

Until then, here are your...

Action Steps

1. Get your vision statement out.

2. Ask yourself: Is my vision balanced? If so, proceed to the next action step. If not, revise your vision statement as necessary before proceeding.

    Reference: Rule 1.

3. Ask yourself: Are the individual components of my vision consistent with one another? If so, proceed to the next action step. If not, revise your vision statement as necessary before proceeding.

    Reference: Rule 2.

4. Ask yourself: Is my vision believable? If so, proceed to the next action step. If not, revise your vision statement as necessary before proceeding.

    Reference: Rule 3.

5. Ask yourself: Is my vision specific? If so, proceed to the next action step. If not, revise your vision statement as necessary before proceeding.

    Reference: Rule 4.

6. Ask yourself: Have you kept your vision confidential? If so, proceed to the next action step. If not, decide what you're going to do about it from this point forward before proceeding.

    Reference: Rule 5.

7. Ask yourself: Is my vision stated in the present tense? If not, revise your vision statement as necessary.

Reference: Rule 6.

Reminder: You may recall, back in the Introduction, I warned you you'd be reevaluating your current next level vision and, possibly, rewriting your vision statement numerous times during the course of these chapters. As frustrating or tedious as it may seem at times, I can assure you, doing so will serve you well now and in the years to come.

Chapter 7: Nine Simple Rules for Wording Your Vision Statement

The purpose of your vision statement is to trigger the experiencing of your vision in your imagination as an already accomplished fact.

In order to do this, it's vitally important for your vision statement to be worded correctly.

There are nine simple rules you absolutely, positively must follow as you design your vision statement to insure your vision statement is worded correctly.

1. You must be in your vision statement.

Use first person pronouns in your vision statement, such as:

- I
- Me
- My

Non-personal, second or third person statements will have little if any effect on your getting what you want.

Remember, the ultimate purpose of writing your vision statement is to get what you want, and the only way that'll happen is with the first person experience in your imagination of already having it, triggered by a first person statement.

Instead of:

"You are earning $10,000 a month..."

Use:

"I am earning $10,000 a month..."

> Note: I'll be using the arbitrary figure of $10,000 a month as an example throughout this chapter. Please don't draw any inference from this. I could just have easily chosen any other number, but this one is easy to work with. That's it.
>
> The income component of your vision statement should reflect what you want and the lifestyle you want to live next in your life.

2. Your vision statement must describe what you want, not what you don't want.

Your vision statement must describe what you want to move *toward*, not what you want to move *away* from.

Instead of:

"I don't make $5,000 a month anymore..."

Use:

"I am earning $10,000 a month..."

3. Your vision statement must be worded in the present tense.

Any reference to the past or future in your vision statement will diminish or destroy the experiential triggering effect of your vision statement.

References to the past will trigger experiences and the accompanying emotions of past appearances – and that isn't what you want to be focusing your attention on.

On the other hand, a vision statement phrased in the future tense always remains in the realm of some day and reinforces the fact you don't have what you want.

Instead of:

"I am making more money than I used to..."

Or...

"I am going to earn $10,000 a month..."

Or...

"I will earn $10,000 a month..."

Use:

"I am earning $10,000 a month..."

4. Your vision statement must say that you already have what you want, not that you're in the process of getting it.

Your vision statement must indicate that you have what you want, not that you're growing into it or progressing toward it.

Your objective is to develop a vision statement that'll easily trigger an imagined experience.

It's much easier to imagine the accomplished result than it is to imagine a changing process.

Instead of:

"My monthly income is steadily increasing..."

Use:

"I am earning $10,000 a month..."

5. Don't compare yourself with others in your vision statement.

Comparing yourself with others opens the door to unconscious acts that might prevent others from getting what they want or, even worse, take something away from others that rightfully belongs to them.

In other words, comparisons might inadvertently cause you to act on the competitive plane rather than on the creative plane.

If you want to earn $10,000 a month as a real estate salesperson...

Instead of:

"I am the #1 real estate salesperson in my company..."

Use:

"I am earning $10,000 a month as a real estate salesperson..."

> Note: The real estate salesperson example above is one that was chosen at random. Please don't draw any inference from it. I could just have easily chosen any other profession to use, but this is the one that popped into my head at the moment. No other reason than that.

Your vision statement should reflect what you want to do to earn the money you want to earn next in your life.

6. Your vision statement must describe your desired result, not your ability to obtain your desired result.

Wording such as "I can" or "I have the ability to" makes your vision difficult to experience in your imagination.

Instead of:

"I can earn $10,000 a month..."

Or...

"I have the ability to earn $10,000 a month..."

Use:

"I am earning $10,000 a month..."

7. Whenever possible, put the positive emotion(s) you want to stimulate right into the wording of your vision statement.

The more dynamic, exciting, vivid, and emotionally charged you make your vision statement, the more effectively it'll serve as a tool to trigger your imaginary experience.

Instead of:

"I am earning $10,000 a month while I..."

Use:

"I am earning $10,000 a month while I enjoy..."

8. In those components of your vision where a specific, measurable result is part of it, don't overshoot in the hope that results may be obtained more rapidly.

In an effort to get what you want even faster, you may be tempted to overstate what you want and, thus, put your vision in the realm of the unimaginable for you right now diminishing or destroying the experiential triggering effect of your vision statement.

If you want to earn $10,000 a month...

Instead of:

"I am earning $100,000 a month..."

Use:

"I am earning $10,000 a month..."

9. Don't build perfection into your vision statement.

Striving for perfection in everything you do isn't only desirable, it's absolutely essential for your success.

However, building perfection into your vision statement will only lead to frustration and, in some cases, it may not be what you really want.

For example, let's say you want to earn a net profit of $10,000 a month from your home-based business.

You might end up earning a net profit of $8,000 one month, $12,000 the next month, $5,000 the month after, and $15,000 the month after that.

Although you'd be averaging a $10,000 a month net profit, if you'd worded your vision statement to make that $10,000 a month a requirement *every* month, you'd be frustrated and feeling as though you were failing at least fifty percent of the time.

Look out for words like:

- Always
- Completely
- Every
- Perfectly

Instead of:

"*I always earn $10,000 a month...*"

Or...

"*I earn $10,000 a month every month...*"

Use:

"*I am earning $10,000 a month...*"

The simplest general rule.

Imagine that you already have what you want in your life, then describe yourself as already having it, keeping it short, sweet, simple, and to the point!

In the next chapter, you'll learn how to use the Monthly Expense Calculator.

Until then, here are your...

Action Steps

1. Get your vision statement out.

2. Ask yourself: Am I in my vision statement? If so, proceed to the next action step. If not, revise your vision statement as necessary before proceeding.

> Reference: Rule 1.

3. Ask yourself: Does my vision statement describe what I want, not what I don't want? If so, proceed to the next action step. If not, revise your vision statement as necessary before proceeding.

> Reference: Rule 2.

4. Ask yourself: Is my vision statement worded in the present tense? If so, proceed to the next action step. If not, revise your vision statement as necessary before proceeding.

> Reference: Rule 3.

5. Ask yourself: Does my vision statement say that I already have what I want, not that I'm in the process of getting it? If so, proceed to the next action step. If not, revise your vision statement as necessary before proceeding.

> Reference: Rule 4.

6. Ask yourself: Do I compare myself with others in my vision statement? If not, proceed to the next action

step. If so, revise your vision statement as necessary before proceeding.

    Reference: Rule 5.

7. Ask yourself: Does my vision statement describe my desired result, not my ability to obtain my desired result? If so, proceed to the next action step. If not, revise your vision statement as necessary before proceeding.

    Reference: Rule 6.

8. Ask yourself: Did I put the positive emotion(s) I want to stimulate right into the wording of my vision statement? If so, proceed to the next action step. If not and if possible, revise your vision statement as necessary before proceeding.

    Reference: Rule 7.

9. Ask yourself: In those components of my vision where a specific, measurable result is part of it, did I overshoot in the hope that results may be obtained more rapidly? If not, proceed to the next action step. If so, revise your vision statement as necessary before proceeding.

    Reference: Rule 8.

10. Ask yourself: Did I build perfection into my vision statement? If so, revise your vision statement.

    Reference: Rule 9.

Extra Credit

Ask yourself: Does my vision statement clearly describe me as already having what I want next in my life, and is it short, sweet, simple, and to the point? If not, revise your vision statement as necessary.

    Reference: The simplest general rule.

Chapter 8: How to Use the Monthly Expense Calculator

In Chapter 7 of my *Wallace D. Wattles Quick Start Guide*, I shared with you how I wrote what I described in the chapter as a "budget in reverse" as part of the process of creating my first vision.

I did it by hand, but a number of years later I came across a great tool that makes the whole process easier and faster, and it does the job better – the Monthly Expense Calculator, which you'll find at:

http://fourhourworkweek.com/expense-calculator

Here's exactly how I suggest you use it to create your vision:

> Note: The instructions below differ somewhat from the instructions that appear on the calculator itself.

1. Input all your current monthly expenses.

The key word here is all. Input *all* your current monthly expenses.

Pay particular attention to expenses you "pay" by credit card.

Believe it or not, there are a whole lot of folks out there who seem to think if they "pay" for something by credit card they haven't spent any money.

Well, just in case you're one of them, guess what? It doesn't work that way!

I highly recommend you go through your last years' worth of credit card statements and put the expenses that appear on them, figured or averaged on a monthly basis, into the appropriate categories of the Monthly Expense Calculator.

All that should appear in the Credit Card Minimum Payments field of the Monthly Expense Calculator is the current monthly total of all your current credit card minimum monthly required payments.

If you have certain quarterly, semiannual, or annual expenses, "paid" by credit card or otherwise, simply prorate these expenses on a monthly basis and enter them into the appropriate category.

For example, if you make a single, annual property tax payment of $1,200 for your car, enter $100 ($1,200 / 12 = $100) into the Property Taxes field of the calculator.

If you have expenses that vary month to month (electricity and heat are two possible examples), I suggest entering the monthly average of the last year.

If a particular expense doesn't neatly fit into any of the calculator's other categories, add it to the Miscellaneous category.

> Note: The more categorized you make your current monthly expenses, the more useful this tool will be to you.

Now, after you've inputted all your current monthly expenses into the appropriate fields of the Monthly

Expense Calculator, click on the Calculate button at the bottom of the calculator.

Then, click on the Print your budget! button at the bottom of the calculator and print your "budget".

You now have a printed snapshot of your outgoing cash flow on a monthly basis.

2. Subtract all nonessentials that're no longer used or used infrequently.

Take a long, hard look at your printed snapshot and ask yourself:

What can I eliminate (the key word here is *eliminate*) that consumes my income and/or attention without enriching my life?

Now, I want you to be real careful here!

I'm not talking about eliminating the brand name green beans you like so much and substituting them with a generic brand of green beans you don't like nearly as much in order to save a dollar a month.

I'm talking about eliminating pure, unadulterated financial waste, things like…

- Subscriptions to magazines you don't read…
- Memberships to services you don't use…
- Seldom driven but often serviced cars…
- Etc.

Here's an example:

A number of years ago, I had two telephone lines coming into my home, one business and one personal. The business line cost roughly $100 a month, the personal line roughly $40 a month.

Now, before we continue, you need to understand that I haven't personally answered a telephone in years nor do I make very many outgoing telephone calls.

So, why, you ask, did I need two telephone lines?

Good question! And, one that I asked myself.

You see, at one time, for a number of reasons, I did, or at least thought I did at the time, need a second business line coming into the house.

However, that time had long passed, and the reasons were no longer valid.

Yet, there I was, continuing to pay $100 a month for something I no longer needed or used.

Why?

I honestly don't know.

Habit, I guess.

Here's the deal:

Odds are there's a whole lot of financial crud you've allowed to build up in your life. Eliminate this financial crud and you'll be well on your way to financing your next level vision.

After you've subtracted all the nonessentials you no longer use or use infrequently, things that consume your income and/or attention without enriching your life, return to the Monthly Expense Calculator and input all your revised monthly expenses into the appropriate fields of the Monthly Expense Calculator.

When you're done, click on the Calculate button at the bottom of the calculator, then click on the Print your budget! button at the bottom of the calculator and print your revised "budget".

You now have a printed snapshot of your outgoing cash flow on a monthly basis minus all the financial crud.

3. Add in the monthly cost(s) of what you want and the lifestyle you want to live next in your life.

Here's a simple example to use as a model:

Let's say you've decided what you want next in your life is a new car and you've picked out the exact make and model you want.

For the sake of simplicity, we'll assume you don't own a car right now.

Through research, you've determined you can own and drive this new car for $600 a month:

- $300 a month for the car payment.
- $100 a month for car insurance.
- $100 a month for property taxes.
- $100 a month for gasoline.

With this information in hand, you'd return to the Monthly Expense Calculator and input all of your revised monthly expenses from Step 2 into the appropriate fields, then:

1. Add $100 in the Property Taxes field.

2. Add $300 in the Car Payments field.

3. Add $100 in the Car Insurance field.

4. Add $100 in the Gasoline field.

Finally, you'd click on the Calculate button at the bottom of the calculator, then click on the Print your budget! button at the bottom of the calculator and, voila, you'd know the exact amount of net monthly income you'd need to get what you want and live the lifestyle you want to live next in your life.

> Tip: Use the number in the Dreamline Buffer field, which provides a 30% buffer, as your net monthly income figure.

Now that you know how much net income you need on a monthly basis to get what you want and live the lifestyle you want to live next in your life, your next step is to determine exactly how much gross income you'll need to earn every month to have the net income necessary to get what you want and live the lifestyle you want to live next in your life.

In the next chapter, I'll show you exactly how to do that.

Until then, here are your...

Action Steps

1. Use the Monthly Expense Calculator to recalculate the income component of your next level vision by following the instructions above, then...

2. Revise your vision statement if necessary.

Chapter 9: How to Use the Gross-Up Calculator

After you've determined exactly how much net income you need on a monthly basis to get what you want and live the lifestyle you want to live next in your life (see the last chapter), your next step is to determine exactly how much gross income you'll need to earn every month to have the net income necessary to get what you want and live the lifestyle you want to live next in your life.

If you live and work in the United States, the easiest way I know of to do this is to use the Gross-Up Calculator, which you'll find at:

http://www.paycheckcity.com/calculator/grossup/

> Note: If you live and work elsewhere, a search of the internet should uncover a similar tool for your area or the information necessary to accomplish the same end manually.
>
> Warning: This site's been a bit finicky as of late. If you have any trouble accessing the Gross-Up Calculator at the link I just gave you, go to http://www.paycheckcity.com and click on Gross Up Calculator near the top of the page. Also, you should know, this site doesn't like ad blockers and, if you use one, you may need to disable it for this site in order to use the calculator.

Now, obviously, there are all sorts of variables to consider. However, in this chapter, I'll walk you through a very simple example you can modify to fit your own situation.

In this particular example, we'll say you've determined you need a net income of $1,500 a month to get what you want and live the lifestyle you want to live next in your life, and:

- The date is 02/29/2016 (which it is at the time of this writing)...

- You live in the state of California...

- You're paid weekly...

- You're single, and...

- You're your only dependent.

Here's how you'd use the Gross-Up Calculator to determine how much gross income you need to earn:

1. Annualize the amount of net income you need on a monthly basis to get what you want and live the lifestyle you want to live next in your life.

To do so, simply multiply your monthly figure times twelve.

In this example, $1,500 a month annualized is $18,000 ($1,500 x 12 = $18,000).

2. Divide this annualized amount by the number of times you're paid in a year.

Since, in this example, you're paid weekly, you're paid fifty-two times a year.

Thus, $18,000 / 52 = $346.15.

3. Go to the Gross-Up Calculator.

Here's the link again:

http://www.paycheckcity.com/calculator/grossup/

> Warning: This site's been a bit finicky as of late. If you have any trouble accessing the Gross-Up Calculator at the link I just gave you, go to http://www.paycheckcity.com and click on Gross Up Calculator near the top of the page. Also, you should know, this site doesn't like ad blockers and, if you use one, you may need to disable it for this site in order to use the calculator.

4. Select 02/29/2016 from the drop-down calendar in the Check Date field under Select Calculation date and state.

Select Calculation date and state	
▶ Check Date	02/29/2016 ▼

5. Select California from the drop-down menu in the State for withholding field under Select Calculation Date and State.

6. Enter $346.15 in the Net Pay field under General Information.

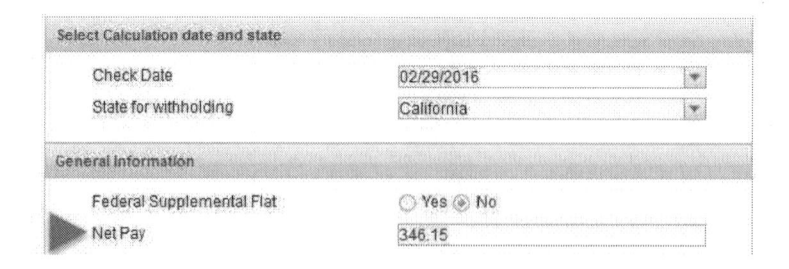

7. Select Weekly from the drop-down menu in the Pay Frequency field under General Information.

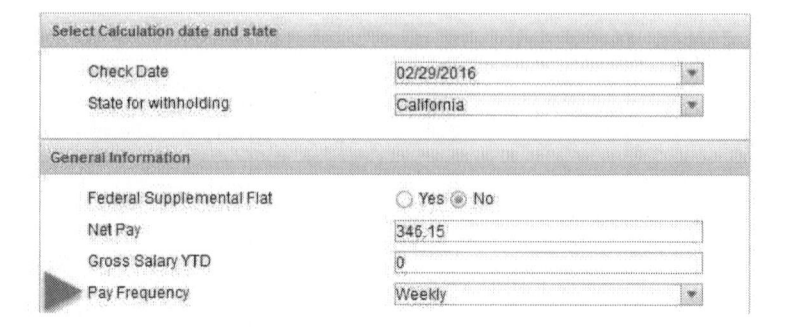

8. Select Single from the drop-down menu in the Federal Filing Status field under General Information.

Select Calculation date and state	
Check Date	02/29/2016
State for withholding	California

General Information	
Federal Supplemental Flat	○ Yes ● No
Net Pay	346.15
Gross Salary YTD	0
Pay Frequency	Weekly
▶ Federal Filing Status	Single

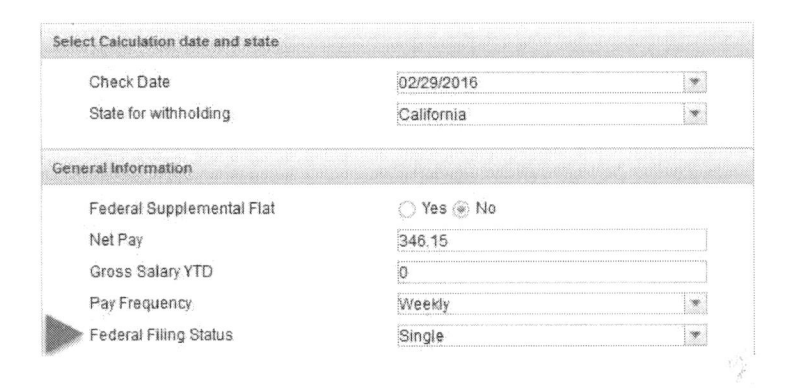

9. Enter 1 in the # of Federal Allowances field under General Information.

Select Calculation date and state	
Check Date	02/29/2016
State for withholding	California

General Information	
Federal Supplemental Flat	○ Yes ● No
Net Pay	346.15
Gross Salary YTD	0
Pay Frequency	Weekly
Federal Filing Status	Single
▶ # of Federal Allowances	1

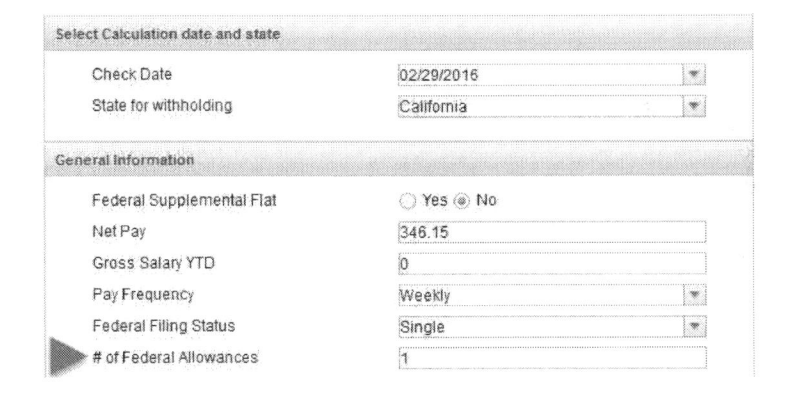

10. Enter 1 in the Regular allowances field under State and Local Information.

Select Calculation date and state	
Check Date	02/29/2016
State for withholding	California

General Information	
Federal Supplemental Flat	○ Yes ● No
Net Pay	346.15
Gross Salary YTD	0
Pay Frequency	Weekly
Federal Filing Status	Single
# of Federal Allowances	1
Additional Federal Withholding	0
Round Federal Withholding	○ Yes ● No
I am exempt from	☐ Federal Tax ☐ FICA ☐ Medicare

State and Local Information	
Additional State Withholding	0
Additional Allowances	0
▶ Regular allowances	1

11. Select Single from the drop-down menu in the Filing Status field under State and Local Information.

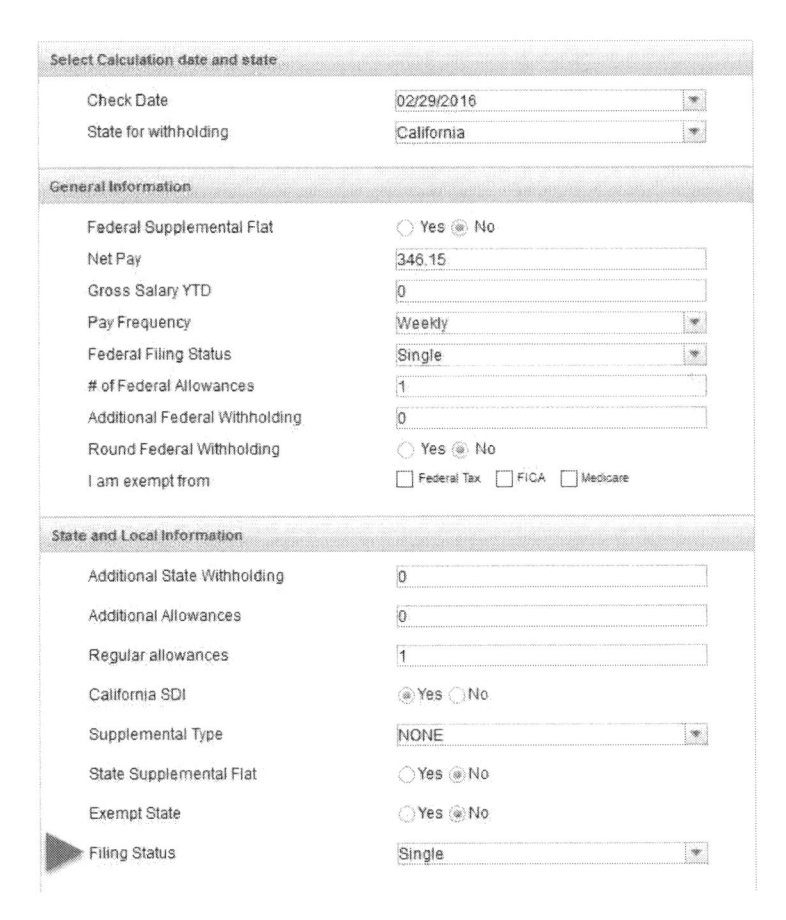

Select Calculation date and state	
Check Date	02/29/2016
State for withholding	California

General Information	
Federal Supplemental Flat	◯ Yes ● No
Net Pay	346.15
Gross Salary YTD	0
Pay Frequency	Weekly
Federal Filing Status	Single
# of Federal Allowances	1
Additional Federal Withholding	0
Round Federal Withholding	◯ Yes ● No
I am exempt from	☐ Federal Tax ☐ FICA ☐ Medicare

State and Local Information	
Additional State Withholding	0
Additional Allowances	0
Regular allowances	1
California SDI	● Yes ◯ No
Supplemental Type	NONE
State Supplemental Flat	◯ Yes ● No
Exempt State	◯ Yes ● No
▶ Filing Status	Single

The Gross-Up Calculator should now look like this:

Select Calculation date and state

Check Date	02/29/2016
State for withholding	California

General Information

Federal Supplemental Flat	○ Yes ⦿ No
Net Pay	346.15
Gross Salary YTD	0
Pay Frequency	Weekly
Federal Filing Status	Single
# of Federal Allowances	1
Additional Federal Withholding	0
Round Federal Withholding	○ Yes ⦿ No
I am exempt from	☐ Federal Tax ☐ FICA ☐ Medicare

State and Local Information

Additional State Withholding	0
Additional Allowances	0
Regular allowances	1
California SDI	⦿ Yes ○ No
Supplemental Type	NONE
State Supplemental Flat	○ Yes ⦿ No
Exempt State	○ Yes ⦿ No
Filing Status	Single

Voluntary Deduction Section

[Add Deduction]   [Remove Deduction]

Deduction #1 Name	
Deduction #1 Amount	
Deduction #1 Type	% of Gross Pay
Ded. #1 Exempt from	☐ Federal ☐ Fica ☐ State ☐ Local

[Calculate]   [Clear]

12. Click on the Calculate button at the bottom of the Gross-Up Calculator.

Select Calculation date and state	
Check Date	02/29/2016
State for withholding	California
General Information	
Federal Supplemental Flat	○ Yes ● No
Net Pay	346.15
Gross Salary YTD	0
Pay Frequency	Weekly
Federal Filing Status	Single
# of Federal Allowances	1
Additional Federal Withholding	0
Round Federal Withholding	○ Yes ● No
I am exempt from	☐ Federal Tax ☐ FICA ☐ Medicare
State and Local Information	
Additional State Withholding	0
Additional Allowances	0
Regular allowances	1
California SDI	● Yes ○ No
Supplemental Type	NONE
State Supplemental Flat	○ Yes ● No
Exempt State	○ Yes ● No
Filing Status	Single
Voluntary Deduction Section	
Add Deduction	Remove Deduction
Deduction #1 Name	
Deduction #1 Amount	
Deduction #1 Type	% of Gross Pay
Ded. #1 Exempt from	☐ Federal ☐ Fica ☐ State ☐ Local
▶ Calculate	Clear

99

The Gross-Up Calculator should now look like this:

Your Paycheck Results

Weekly Gross Pay	$422.07
Federal Withholding	$36.22
Social Security	$26.17
Medicare	$6.12
California	$3.61
SDI	$3.80

Net Pay

Net Pay	$346.15

Calculation Based On

Check Date	02/29/2016
Gross Pay	$0.00
Gross Salary YTD	$0.00
Pay Frequency	Weekly
Federal Filing Status	Single
# of Federal Allowances	1
Additional Federal Withholding	$0.00
State for withholding	California
Additional State Withholding	0
Additional Allowances	0
Regular allowances	1
California SDI	true
Supplemental Type	NONE
State Supplemental Flat	false
Exempt State	false
Filing Status	S

[New Calculation]   [Print Options]

13. Look at the results under Your Pay Check Results.

Your Paycheck Results

Weekly Gross Pay	$422.07
Federal Withholding	$36.22
Social Security	$26.17
Medicare	$6.12
California	$3.61
SDI	$3.80

As you can see on the Weekly Gross Pay line, you need to earn a gross income of $422.07 a week in order to take home $346.15 a week.

```
Your Paycheck Results
Weekly Gross Pay         $422.07
Federal Withholding       $36.22
Social Security           $26.17
Medicare                   $6.12
California                 $3.61
SDI                        $3.80
```

14. Multiply $422.07 times 52 (the number of times you're paid in a year) to annualize it.

$422.07 x 52 = $21,947.64.

15. Divide $21,947.64 by 12 (the number of months in a year).

$21947.64 / 12 = $1,828.97.

And there you have it, in order to have a net income of $1,500 a month to get what you want and live the lifestyle you want to live next in your life, you need to earn a gross income of $1,828.97 a month.

> Note: For any one of a large number of reasons, this number may change over time. However, it provides a useful starting point for the purpose of writing your vision statement.

A couple of important points:

First, this calculator changes from time to time. However, the essentials of using it usually remain the same.

So, should this calculator have changed when you go to use it, simply adapt the above instructions to the change and you should be just fine.

Second, there are way too many variables, self-employment being but one of them, to cover every possible situation in this chapter.

If your situation falls outside the scope of this chapter and you're having trouble determining how much gross income you need to earn a certain amount of net income, I suggest one of two things:

    1. Consult a competent accounting or tax professional, or...

    2. Just estimate it and move on.

Frankly, preferring to keep it simple, I opt for the latter. I double the amount of net income I desire and use that figure as my gross income figure.

For some that would be a gross overestimation, for others a gross underestimation, but, for me, all factors considered, it works out just about right.

In the next chapter, you'll learn how to incorporate debt elimination into your next level vision the right way.

Until then, here are your...

Action Steps

1. Use the Gross-Up Calculator, its equivalent, or one of the other methods mentioned to recalculate the income component of your next level vision, then...

2. Revise your vision statement if necessary.

Chapter 10: Purpose and Debt

A while back, I received a question, actually two very closely related questions, from a customer that went something like this:

> Note: I edited out the personal details and slightly edited the questions to reflect several other very similar questions I've received.

"Hi Tony, I'm hoping you can help me out with something. I've read The Science of Getting Rich by Wallace D. Wattles quite a number of times now and I have a question regarding one part.

In Chapter 8 of The Science of Getting Rich, it says...

'And by prayer I mean holding steadily to your vision, with the purpose to cause its creation into solid form, and the faith that you are doing so.'

By 'purpose', did Wallace D. Wattles mean the reason or reasons why you want something?

If that's correct, I want to be free and clear, meaning I don't want to owe anyone any money at all. So, I'm thinking about and visualizing how nice and calm it would be to not owe anyone any money, to not have to pay anything off, to have the money I make after bills and taxes to be pure profit, to be able to have that extra money to save or buy things as I wish. To have the feeling of being completely financially secure and be at the point that I actually don't need any extra money.

The thing I'm confused about is I know I shouldn't be thinking about getting out of debt as I'm then thinking about debt which I know is wrong. So, how do I think about not being in debt without thinking about debt?"

Excellent questions!

Let's start with the first one:

"By 'purpose', did Wallace D. Wattles mean the reason or reasons why you want something?"

Mr. Wattles' use of the word purpose as it relates to vision had me puzzled for the longest time, but I finally figured it out.

Simply substitute the word intention for the word purpose.

Thus...

"And by prayer I mean holding steadily to your vision, with the purpose to cause its creation into solid form, and the faith that you are doing so."

Becomes...

And by prayer I mean holding steadily to your vision, with the intention to cause its creation into solid form, and the faith that you are doing so.

When you look at it this way, the attainment of your vision, in and of itself, becomes your purpose, so to speak.

Now, with that in mind...

"... I know I shouldn't be thinking about getting out of debt as I am then thinking about debt..."

Absolutely correct!

It's near impossible to think about getting out of debt without thinking about what?

Debt, right?

And, as I'm sure you know by now, if that's what you're thinking about, that's exactly what you'll have in your life... debt.

"So, how do I think about not being in debt without thinking about debt?"

Simple.

Stop thinking about debt altogether.

Here's what I suggest:

Create a clear, concise, definite vision of what you want next in your life that includes earning a specific amount of income that's adequate for getting what you want next while living a debt-free lifestyle (the first step to getting out of debt is to stop incurring new debts) and includes an allowance for systematically (the key word here is *systematically*) paying off your existing debts.

Then, once you have that in place, focus *all* your attention on earning that amount of income and getting what you want next, allowing the debt to take care of itself, so to speak.

Here's an example:

> Note: This example comes from Chapter 3 of this guide. I suggest rereading it before continuing with this chapter.

Shannon is twenty years old and living at home with her parents. She recently dropped out of college and isn't working.

Obviously, Shannon's parents were disappointed in her decision to leave school because they'd really like to see her make something of herself.

And, they're not alone. Shannon would really like to make something of herself too! The trouble is she's not sure what.

You see, like a lot of folks, Shannon feels sort of lost. She knows she wants more out of life, but she's just not sure what. However, she does know what's important to her right now.

She'd like to have a full-time job so she'll have income of her own.

Up until now, other than a few odd part-time jobs while she was going to school, she's been dependent on her parents for her financial needs and wants.

Since she doesn't know exactly what she wants to do, she's not real fussy as to the kind of job right now as long as it's enjoyable to her and not illegal or immoral.

Shannon would also like to own her own car. She's been using her mother's car as she needs it, but she'd really like the independence of having her own car.

Although she doesn't know specifically which make and model right now, she does know she wants to buy or lease a new car, not a used car.

Eventually, she'd also like to move out of her parent's home and live on her own, but this isn't a high priority for her right now.

So, right now, Shannon's highest priorities, her top values (see Chapter 1 of this guide for details) are:

1. An enjoyable job.

2. Owning a new car.

Now that she's clear about what's most important to her, Shannon's next step is to determine specifically what she wants next in her life and the exact amount of income she'll need to get what she wants and live the life she wants to live next.

For starters, she wants to own a new car. So, she goes car shopping and picks out a make and model she likes.

Shannon learns she can lease the car she likes, with no money down, for $300 a month. She also learns it'll cost her $100 a month for car insurance and another $100 a month for property taxes on the car.

Shannon now knows that to get her new car, she'll need $500 a month in income to pay for it ($300 a month for the lease payment + $100 a month for car insurance + $100 a month for property taxes = $500 a month).

In addition, Shannon's in credit card and student loan debt to the tune of $5,000, $2,500 in credit card debt and $2,500 in student loan debt.

Her minimum required payment on her credit card debt is $100 a month, and her minimum required payment on her student loan debt is $50 a month, both of which she's currently paying by borrowing from Peter to pay Paul, digging herself into the hole even further.

She's decided as soon as she starts working and has income, she's going to pay for whatever she wants by cash, check, debit card, or electronic transfer. No more charging anything!

And, since she doesn't want to be in debt forever, she's decided she wants to pay an extra $50 a month, over and above the minimum required payments due, to pay off her debts faster.

She's decided to start by applying the $50 a month to her credit card debt as it has the highest interest rate.

> Note: I used to teach, because it's exactly what I did to get out of debt, to pay off debts with the highest interest rates first. However, since then, I discovered a far easier and faster way of going about it that we'll get to shortly.

So, there's another $200 a month in income she'll need ($150 a month to make the minimum required payments + $50 a month for debt elimination = $200 a month).

Then, Shannon wants to have some spending money for clothes, eating out, gas for her new car, going out, etc. She determines that $400 a month will be adequate for that right now.

Plus, besides helping around the house, which she's been doing, Shannon wants to give her parents $100 a month room and board, which they've agreed to and intend on saving for her.

Let's summarize, to get what she wants and live the life she wants to live next, Shannon needs to earn:

- $100 a month for room and board.

- $100 a month for property taxes for her car.

- $150 a month for credit card payments ($100 a month for the minimum required payment + $50 a month for debt elimination).

- $300 a month for her car payment.

- $50 a month for her minimum required student loan payment.

- $100 a month for car insurance.

- $400 a month to spend anyway she likes.

Plugging these numbers into the appropriate categories of the Monthly Expense Calculator at:

http://fourhourworkweek.com/expense-calculator

Shannon determines that, with a 30% buffer, she needs to earn a total of $1,560 a month.

> Note: In Chapter 8 of this guide, you got detailed, step-by-step instructions for using the Monthly Expense Calculator.

However, she really needs to earn more than that, doesn't she?

Why?

Simple.

Living in the United States and in a state that has an income tax, Shannon must take into account federal and state income, Medicare, and Social Security taxes that'll be deducted from what she earns.

In reality, to take home $1,560 a month, using the Gross-Up Calculator at:

http://www.paycheckcity.com/calculator/grossup/

> Warning: This site's been a bit finicky as of late. If you have any trouble accessing the Gross-Up Calculator at the link I just gave you, go to http://www.paycheckcity.com and click on Gross Up Calculator near the top of the page. Also, you should know, this site doesn't like ad blockers and, if you use one, you may need to disable it for this site in order to use the calculator.

Shannon determines she'll need to earn $1,927.99 a month gross income (Shannon lives in the state of California, is single, is her own dependent, and is assuming, at this point, she'll be paid weekly).

> Note: Due to changes in tax rates and other variables, this amount may be different than what the calculator would return today.

> Note: In Chapter 9 of this guide, you got detailed, step-by-step instructions for using the Gross-Up Calculator.

> Note: Because it's where I live and the system I work under, I write from the perspective of United States tax laws (the only ones I have any firsthand knowledge of) when discussing the issue of taking taxes into consideration when determining the gross amount of income you must earn to take home a specific amount of net income.

If you live and work outside of the United States, you'll need to make this calculation based on your country's tax laws and/or whatever else might be deducted from your gross income where you live. With a little searching on the internet you might be able to find tools like the Gross-Up Calculator to help you. It's the principle that's important here not the specific tool or technique.

Shannon rounds this figure up to $2,000 a month.

So, what Shannon wants next in her life is to earn $2,000 a month from a job she enjoys and to have a new car, thus her vision statement reads:

"I am earning $2,000 a month from a job I enjoy while I enjoy driving my new _____."

Following the instructions in my *Wallace D. Wattles Quick Start Guide*, Shannon obtains these things in a few months.

Now, let's take a detailed, step-by-step look at exactly what Shannon did to get out of debt:

1. Shannon created a clear, concise, definite vision of what she wanted next in her life that included earning a specific amount of monthly income that was adequate for getting what she wanted next while living a debt-free lifestyle and included an allowance for systematically paying off her existing debts.

There are three important things I want you to note here:

First, Shannon didn't approach this step from the perspective of being in debt, nor that of getting out of debt. She approached it based solely on what was important to her at the time, her values, and what she wanted next in her life, PERIOD!

> Note: For more information on values, see Chapter 1 of this guide.
>
> Note: See Chapters 6, 7, and 8 of my *Wallace D. Wattles Quick Start Guide* and the chapters of this guide for the details of vision creation.

In other words, other than the specific monthly income required for getting what she wanted next while living a debt-free lifestyle, her vision would have been exactly the same regardless of whether or not she was in debt.

Second, Shannon calculated exactly what it was going to cost her every single month to get what she wanted and live the lifestyle she wanted to live next in her life without incurring more debt to do so.

Note: Although it could be construed as such, as a leased car has to be returned at the end of its lease period, I look at car lease payments as a bill rather than a debt, no different than when renting or leasing an apartment, condo, or home for example.

Right here is where most folks fall down. They either grossly underestimate or out-and-out lie to themselves about what things really cost and/or the effect of taxes on their bottom line income.

They're running around out there trying to live a $5,000 a month lifestyle, let's say, on $4,000 a month net income, financing their deficit on their credit cards and/or home equity loans, all the while thinking they're doing better than they really are.

Don't let that be you!

When creating your next level vision be brutally honest with yourself about what things are really going to cost you and how much income you really have to earn to afford them without going into debt.

Here's a tip:

Whatever you think something's going to cost you, odds are it's going to cost you more. Now, I fully realize that sounds a tad negative. However, that's the way it is.

If you own a car or a home, you know exactly what I'm talking about here.

So, since that's the way it is, the prudent thing to do is plan for it in advance.

> Note: One of the things I like about Tim Ferriss' Monthly Expense Calculator as a next level vision planning tool is that it automatically builds in a thirty-percent buffer that can be used for covering unexpected expenses and/or building up your surplus (before this calculator was available, I did this manually). I like to refer to this buffer as my built in abundance factor.

Third, Shannon has a simple, unobtrusive system in place that'll allow her to begin eliminating her existing debts as soon as she has income coming in (making the best use of what she has), that doesn't require her to pinch pennies, get a second job, or cut back her spending in any way (all of which foster an attitude of lack, which is exactly what you don't want), yet still allows her to become debt free in a relatively short period of time while she's in the process of getting what she wants next.

Let's take a closer look at the debt-elimination system she set up.

> Note: This is the way I teach it now.

Shannon's total debt is $5,000 on which her minimum required monthly payments total $150. It breaks down as follows:

- Credit Card 1 – $500 balance, $20 minimum required monthly payment.

- Credit Card 2 – $750 balance, $30 minimum required monthly payment.

- Credit Card 3 – $1,250 balance, $50 minimum required monthly payment.

- Student Loan – $2,500 balance, $50 minimum required monthly payment.

As stated in the example above, Shannon's decided to pay an extra $50 a month, over and above the minimum required payments due, to pay off these debts faster.

> Note: At least one person I know refers to this specific amount of money you have every month extra to add to your debt elimination program as your "head start money".

What does she do with this extra $50 payment every month?

She starts by making a prioritized list of each of her debts in ascending order by balance owed (not the minimum required monthly payment), from the lowest balance owed to the highest balance owed, and notes the minimum required monthly payment for each.

> Note: If Shannon had a car payment, for a purchased car as opposed to a leased car, and/or a home mortgage payment, she'd add those to this list the same exact way.

For example:

1. Credit Card 1 – $500 balance, $20 minimum required monthly payment.

2. Credit Card 2 – $750 balance, $30 minimum required monthly payment.

3. Credit Card 3 – $1,250 balance, $50 minimum required monthly payment.

4. Student Loan – $2,500 balance, $50 minimum required monthly payment.

Then, as soon as she has income coming in, she adds this extra $50 a month to the minimum required monthly payment of the first debt on her list, the one with the lowest balance, continuing to make the minimum required monthly payments for the remaining debts on her list.

In other words, instead of making a $20 payment on Credit Card 1 every month, the debt she owes the least on, she makes a $70 payment ($20 minimum required monthly payment + $50 a month extra for debt elimination = $70 a month) while she continues making the minimum required monthly payments on Credit Card 2, Credit Card 3, and her Student Loan.

> Note: Should her minimum required monthly payment be lowered as she pays down the balance on Credit Card 1, she'd continue paying the $70 a month.

Then, and this is key, once Credit Card 1 is paid off in full, Shannon takes the $70 a month she was paying on Credit Card 1 and adds it to the minimum required monthly payment for Credit Card 2, the debt with the second lowest balance, continuing to make the minimum required monthly payments for the remaining debts on her list.

In other words, instead of making a $30 payment on Credit Card 2 every month, the debt she now owes the least on with Credit Card 1 out of the way, she makes a $100 payment ($30 minimum required monthly payment + $70 a month extra for debt elimination = $100 a month) while she continues making the minimum required monthly payments on Credit Card 3 and her Student Loan.

> Note: Should her minimum required monthly payment be lowered as she pays down the balance on Credit Card 2, she'd continue paying the $100 a month.

Then...

Starting to get the picture?

Good.

When Credit Card 2 is paid off in full, Shannon takes the $100 a month she was paying on Credit Card 2 and adds it to the minimum required monthly payment for Credit Card 3, the debt with the third lowest balance, continuing to make the minimum required monthly payment for the remaining debt on her list.

In other words, instead of making a $50 payment on Credit Card 3 every month, the debt she now owes the least on with Credit Card 1 and Credit Card 2 out of the way, she makes a $150 payment ($50 minimum required monthly payment + $100 a month extra for debt elimination = $150 a month) while she continues making the minimum required monthly payment on her Student Loan.

> Note: Should her minimum required monthly payment be lowered as she pays down the balance on Credit Card 3, she'd continue paying the $150 a month.

Then...

Guess what?

You got it!

When Credit Card 3 is paid off in full, Shannon takes the $150 a month she was paying on Credit Card 3 and adds it to the minimum required monthly payment for her Student Loan, the debt with the highest balance.

In other words, instead of making a $50 payment on her Student Loan every month, her only remaining debt with Credit Card 1, Credit Card 2, and Credit Card 3 out of the way, she makes a $200 payment ($50 minimum required monthly payment + $150 a month extra for debt elimination = $200 a month).

> Note: Should her minimum required monthly payment be lowered as she pays down the balance on her Student Loan, she'd continue paying the $200 a month.

That's it. That's all there was to her system.

And once it was in place, from that point on...

2. Shannon focused all (the key word here is *all*) her attention on earning the amount of income her vision called for and getting what she wanted next in her life, allowing the debt to take care of itself, so to speak.

She didn't talk about debt, she didn't think about debt, she focused her attention solely on what she wanted next in her life and imagined herself as already having it.

As a result, within a few short months, Shannon had the job, she had the income, she had the car, she had the debt-free lifestyle, and, shortly thereafter, she was one-hundred percent, totally debt free!

Whoa bucko, how'd that happen so fast?

Simple...

First, just as she had intended to do, as soon as she had some income coming in, Shannon began paying for whatever she bought by cash, check, debit card, or electronic transfer.

In other words, she immediately began living a debt-free lifestyle.

Sadly, most folks never quite figure this absolutely vital first step out. They're trying to eliminate debt on one end while, at the very same time, adding to it on the other. Don't let that be you!

Second, Shannon had, and took advantage of, the opportunity to work a lot of overtime over a period of several months and very wisely added the extra money she earned by working the overtime every month to the extra payment she was making on her lowest balance debt at the time, thus making her system work all that much faster.

One very important thing I want to point out here...

Once you have this system in place and get some momentum going with it, I can tell you from personal experience, a snowball effect will begin to develop and all sorts of opportunities, not necessarily in the way of overtime as it did for Shannon, will come to you to make it happen even faster without taking away from what you want or the lifestyle you want to live.

They did for Shannon, they did for me, and they will for you too!

With that, I'd like to leave you with this. It comes from *The Art of Money Getting or Golden Rules for Making Money* by P.T. Barnum:

"Debt robs a man of his self-respect, and makes him almost despise himself. Grunting and groaning and working for what he has eaten up or worn out, and now when he is called upon to pay up, he has nothing to show for his money; this is properly termed 'working for a dead horse.'"

How absolutely true!

However, it doesn't have to be that way. You don't have to "work for a dead horse" forever. There's a way out, a right way out, and you now know exactly what it is.

So, go to it and do it!

In the next chapter, you'll learn what to do when you don't know what you want until you do know what you want.

Until then, here are your...

Action Steps

1. Reread Chapter 2 of this guide.

2. Ask yourself: Should I be focusing on financial stability or debt elimination, if either, right now?

3. In light of the above and what you learned from this chapter, reevaluate your next level vision, then...

4. Refine or revise it as necessary.

Chapter 11: What to Do Until You Know What You Want

What do you do when you don't know what you want until you do know what you want?

Good question.

And, fortunately, one to which Wallace D. Wattles gave us the answer.

In Lesson 10 of his book *The Personal Power Course* ("Opportunity"), he wrote:

"... Nature is a Living Intelligence, and that this intelligence is all-powerful within its domain; and perhaps you have not fully grasped this in all that it means to you. Every living thing has intelligence after its own kind, and according to its form; but there is an Unformed Intelligence in all, through all, and permeating all; and this Unformed Intelligence is moving always toward more life for all.

This Intelligence being the source of all things, knows the real truth concerning all things; and when you come in touch with It you will have what is called an intuitive perception of truth; you will discover things. Things will open before your mind. It will not be hard for you to think of new ways, and new things to do, as described in the foregoing. If you get into the mental attitude of FAITH and ACTION described in these lessons, you are not going to have to painfully cudgel at your brain to discover something to do; you will be led to it, or it will be brought to you. Do not suppose that it is very difficult to invent new things, or to discover new methods; the new ways are already known, and you only need to come in touch with Mind which knows them. All that is necessary is that with absolute FAITH, you should do all that you can do NOW, and keep moving toward more life. It does not in the least matter that you cannot see the big thing you are to do; it will be shown to you, in due time, for there is ONE who knows. Have faith, and MOVE ON."

And therein lies the answer...

Simply put:

Have faith and move on!

Have faith that what you want, what you're to do next in your life, will be revealed to you when the time is right while, at the same time, doing all that you can do now and moving forward toward more life.

There are going to be times in your life when it's going to be real difficult for you to figure out exactly what you want next in your life.

More often than not, it's going be right after you've reached one of your next level visions.

That happened to me after my first couple of visions became my reality.

After my business income increased to the point where I could stay self-employed and I wasn't struggling financially anymore, I was spending unlimited time with my son, I had the car, I had the home, and my health was improving, quite frankly, I was really rather comfortable at that point and didn't know what, if anything, I wanted next in my life.

So, what did I do?

I did exactly as Mr. Wattles said to do. I continued doing all that I could do each day, doing each separate thing in an efficient manner, moving forward toward more life, with the full faith that what I was to do next in my life would be revealed to me when the time was right for me to know it.

And guess what?

It was!

And, as a result, we're both here today.

So, if you really don't know what you want next in your life, don't get upset about it, don't beat yourself over it, simply have faith and move on.

It *will* come to you!

In the next chapter, you'll learn how long it'll take to get what you want.

Until then, here are your...

Action Steps

1. Reread this passage from Lesson 10 of *The Personal Power Course*:

"... Nature is a Living Intelligence, and that this intelligence is all-powerful within its domain; and perhaps you have not fully grasped this in all that it means to you. Every living thing has intelligence after its own kind, and according to its form; but there is an Unformed Intelligence in all, through all, and permeating all; and this Unformed Intelligence is moving always toward more life for all.

This Intelligence being the source of all things, knows the real truth concerning all things; and when you come in touch with It you will have what is called an intuitive perception of truth; you will discover things. Things will open before your mind. It will not be hard for you to think of new ways, and new things to do, as described in the foregoing. If you get into the mental attitude of FAITH and ACTION described in these lessons, you are not going to have to painfully cudgel at your brain to discover something to do; you will be led to it, or it will be brought to you. Do not suppose that it is very difficult to invent new things, or to discover new methods; the new ways are already known, and you only need to come in touch with Mind which knows them. All that is necessary is that with absolute FAITH, you should do all that you can do NOW, and keep moving toward more life. It does not in the least matter that you cannot see the big thing you are to do; it will be shown to you, in due time, for there is ONE who knows. Have faith, and MOVE ON."

Then...

2. Write down, in your own words, what this passage means to you and specifically how you'll apply it from this point forward.

> Tip: Spend some serious time reading, rereading, and pondering this passage. It'll be time well spent.

Chapter 12: How Long Will It Take to Get What You Want?

I'm frequently asked:

"How long will it take to get what I want?"

And, my answer is always the same.

It's the exact same answer I used to give my son when he asked me how long something was going to take (which, I might add, was rather frequently).

Are you ready?

Here it is:

It's going to take however long it's going to take!

You see, how long it's going to take to get what you want isn't for you to know.

You don't know all the things or combinations of things that may be necessary for you to get what you want.

If you did, odds are you'd already have it, wouldn't you?

In Chapter 12 of *The Science of Getting Rich* ("Efficient Action"), Mr. Wattles wrote:

"... you do not know the workings of all the forces that have been set moving in your behalf... You can never know all the combinations which Supreme Intelligence is making for you in the world of things and of human affairs..."

Here's the deal:

After you've decided what you want and have a clear mental picture of yourself already enjoying it, the key is faith.

Faith is what makes the impression on the Formless.

You must have complete, one-hundred percent, absolute, total, unwavering faith not only that what you want is going to happen but it's happening now, right now!

The only questions are when and how you'll see what you want.

And those things aren't up to you to decide.

They're up to the Universe.

In the meantime, you must do all you can do each day, doing each separate act in the most perfect manner possible.

Regardless of appearances to the contrary and no matter what happens or goes on around you, it's absolutely critical for you to keep your faith and to keep acting constructively.

What you want will come when the time is right for you to have it.

Just know it will!

Here are your...

Action Steps

1. Reread this passage from Chapter 12 of *The Science of Getting Rich*:

"... you do not know the workings of all the forces that have been set moving in your behalf... You can never know all the combinations which Supreme Intelligence is making for you in the world of things and of human affairs..."

Then...

2. Write down, in your own words, what this passage means to you and specifically how you'll apply it from this point forward.

Conclusion

Well, there you have my *Wallace D. Wattles Advanced Vision Guide*.

It's been an absolute pleasure sharing this life-changing information with you, and I look forward to the day we can do it again.

Thanks again for taking the time to purchase this book!

If you enjoyed this book, please take the time to leave me a review on Amazon. I appreciate your honest feedback, and it really helps me to continue producing high-quality books.

Also, don't forget to grab your copy of the free bonus I mentioned at the start of this book! If you haven't already, head to http://bit.ly/2hnJZEM to access it.

I sincerely hope you found this book to be helpful and wish you the absolute best with your study and application of Mr. Wattles' writings! If you're interested in learning more about his writings and how to apply them to your life, I invite you to take a look at my blog. You can do so by going to http://www.tonymase.com.

Once again, thanks for taking the time to purchase this book!

To your success,

Tony Mase
http://www.tonymase.com

Appendix: Resources

Links to resources you might find helpful.

Gross-Up Calculator

If you live and work in the United States and work for someone else, you can use this calculator to determine how much gross income you need to earn a specific amount of net income. It defaults to Arizona, but the state can be changed in one of the drop-down menus.

http://www.paycheckcity.com/calculator/grossup/

> Warning: This site's been a bit finicky as of late. If you have any trouble accessing the Gross-Up Calculator at the link I just gave you, go to http://www.paycheckcity.com and click on Gross Up Calculator near the top of the page. Also, you should know, this site doesn't like ad blockers and, if you use one, you may need to disable it for this site in order to use the calculator.

Monthly Expense Calculator

You can use this calculator to calculate your total current monthly expenses, find and eliminate financial clutter, and determine the exact monthly cost of your next level vision.

http://fourhourworkweek.com/expense-calculator

Oxford Advanced American Dictionary

The *Oxford Advanced American Dictionary* is one of several dictionaries I use in my study of Mr. Wattles' writings. Although intended for learners of the English language, I like its simple definitions and clear, concise examples.

http://oaadonline.oxfordlearnersdictionaries.com

Salary Paycheck Calculator

If you live and work in the United States and work for someone else, you can use this calculator to estimate your net or take-home pay after taxes and deductions are withheld from your gross salary. It defaults to Arizona, but the state can be changed in one of the dropdown menus.

http://www.paycheckcity.com/calculator/salary/

> Warning: This site's been a bit finicky as of late. If you have any trouble accessing the Salary Calculator at the link I just gave you, go to http://www.paycheckcity.com and click on Salary Calculator near the top of the page. Also, you should know, this site doesn't like ad blockers and, if you use one, you may need to disable it for this site in order to use the calculator.

Wallace D. Wattles Quick Start Guide

The *Wallace D. Wattles Quick Start Guide* is designed to help you begin creating wealth, health, success, happiness, and love in your life using Wallace D. Wattles' principles... starting today!

http://amzn.to/1mT6Er7

About Wallace D. Wattles

Unfortunately, although he wrote some of the most powerful, life-changing books and articles ever written, very little is known about the life of Wallace D. Wattles.

We do know he was born in the United States around 1860 and experienced a life of failure after failure, until, in his later years, after tireless study and experimentation, he formulated and put into practice the philosophy he later wrote about in his books and articles.

Perhaps the most accurate portrait we have of the man, one that tells us what's truly important to know about him, was written by his daughter Florence in a letter to Elizabeth Towne, his primary publisher, shortly after his untimely passing in 1911.

Here are excerpts from that touching letter, which were published in a later edition of Mr. Wattles' book *The Science of Being Great*:

"My dear Mrs. Towne:

Your letter of the 14th received... perhaps a little later I can write the romantic story of my Father's life and make it really worthwhile.

You knew, didn't you, that he lost a good position in the Methodist Church because of his 'heresy'? He met George D. Herron at a convention of reformers in Chicago in 1896 and caught Herron's social vision. I shall never forget the morning he came home. It was Christmas. Mother had put her last dollar into a cuff box and we had placed it beneath an evergreen branch which served for our Christmas tree and which we had illuminated with tallow candles and strung with popcorn. Finally Father came. With that beautiful smile he praised the tree, said the cuff box was just what he had been wanting – and took us all in his arms to tell us of the wonderful social message of Jesus, the message which he later embodied in 'A New Christ'. From that day until his death he worked unceasingly to realize the glorious vision of human brotherhood.

For years his life was cursed by poverty and the fear of poverty. He was always scheming and planning to get for his family those things which make the abundant life possible. In the first chapter of 'The Science of Getting Rich' he says: 'A man's highest happiness is found in the bestowal of benefits on those he loves.' The supreme faith of the man never left him; never for a moment did he lose confidence in the power of the master Intelligence to right every wrong and to give to every man and woman his or her share of the good things of life.

When we came to Elwood (Indiana) three years ago, Father began a Sunday night lectureship in Indianapolis. This was our only source of income. Later he began to write for Nautilus and to word out his own philosophy. He wrote almost constantly. Then it was that he formed his mental picture. He saw himself as a successful writer, a personality of power, an advancing man, and he began to work toward the realization of this vision... He lived every page of 'The Science of Being Great'. In the last three years he made lots of money, and had good health, except for his extreme frailty.

I have written this hurriedly, but I think it will give you an idea of the life struggle of a great man – his failure and success. His life was truly THE POWERFUL LIFE, and surely we can say, at least in Elwood, 'The name of him who loved his fellow men led all the rest.'

With all good wishes, I am,

Very sincerely,

FLORENCE A. WATTLES"

Although very little is known about his life, I, like so very many others who've studied and applied his philosophy over the years, am so very grateful Wallace D. Wattles lived and wrote it down.

About Tony Mase

I'm a serious student of the works of Wallace D. Wattles, who's best known for his classic masterpiece *The Science of Getting Rich*. I discovered his writings (or they discovered me) in 1998 and used what I learned from them to make more progress over the next couple of years – both personally and in business – than I did in the previous thirty years combined.

Nowadays, though I don't really look at it as such, I spend the vast majority of my allotted "work" time helping other people do the same through the books I publish.

I absolutely love sharing Mr. Wattles' writings with people and advising them on how to apply his philosophy to their lives. I enjoy seeing their self-imposed shackles fall by the wayside and their true selves rise to the surface. I sincerely hope I was able to do that with the book you're holding in your hands and that you've enjoyed reading it every bit as much as I did putting it together.

I regularly post practical self-development information and updates to my blog and Twitter.

Check out my blog at http://www.tonymase.com.

Follow me on Twitter at https://twitter.com/tonymasenews.

Other Books from Tony Mase

I hope you enjoyed this book! I have some other titles available on Amazon that I think you may be interested in. Below is a list of my other books along with direct links to their pages on Amazon.

- A Second Courtship: http://amzn.to/1uY9BX0

- Courtship by Absent Treatment: http://amzn.to/10in3un

- Fundamentals Bundle: http://amzn.to/1fjgMRD

- God: The Servant of Humanity: http://amzn.to/1po3O76

- How to Get What You Want: http://amzn.to/13zTsXo

- How Wallace D. Wattles Got Rich and How You Can Too!: http://amzn.to/22WMPPS

- Lessons in Constructive Science: http://amzn.to/1eWrX3I

- Making the Man or Woman Who Can: http://amzn.to/16kkgfx

- Marital Unhappiness: A New Remedy: http://amzn.to/XARcU4

- Mind: What Is It?: http://amzn.to/18zxt5D

- Personal Power Bundle: http://amzn.to/1jUxLyz

- Post-Panic Pragmatics: http://amzn.to/1rwxtEy

- Relationships Bundle: http://amzn.to/1rQQzAG

- Success Bundle: http://amzn.to/1ddrX0E

- The 7 Biggest Mistakes Wallace D. Wattles Readers Make and How to Avoid Them: http://amzn.to/2eP6e7w

- The Law of Opulence: http://amzn.to/1igpAIx

- The Personal Power Course: http://amzn.to/1fiEyke

- The Powerful Life: http://amzn.to/W9Wdmi

- Unity with the Things You Want: http://amzn.to/1qtY83Y

- Wallace D. Wattles Master Collection: http://amzn.to/1SHMMW9

- Wallace D. Wattles Productivity Acceleration Guide: http://amzn.to/1syEfJO

- Wallace D. Wattles Quick Start Guide: http://amzn.to/1mT6Er7

- Wallace D. Wattles' Constructive Living Course: http://amzn.to/2mj3RdN

- Wallace D. Wattles' Health Science Course: http://amzn.to/29bxolw

- Wallace D. Wattles' Marital Happiness Course: http://amzn.to/2aCSyrE

- Wallace D. Wattles' Power Correspondence School Courses Bundle: http://amzn.to/2cmCaJH

- Wallace D. Wattles' Talent Development Course: http://amzn.to/2bh1VNg

- Wallace D. Wattles' Wealth Science Course: http://amzn.to/2aqgONZ

- What Is Truth?: http://amzn.to/1bcANrI

For my latest offerings and updates, please visit my blog at http://www.tonymase.com.